Racism, Islamophobia,
Antisemitism and the Future
of Canadian Society

S.D. Clark

The University of Toronto's Department of Sociology was established in 1963. Samuel Delbert (S.D.) Clark (1910–2003) was its founding Chair.

Clark was born in Lloydminster, Alberta, and attended the University of Saskatchewan, the London School of Economics, McGill University and the University of Toronto. He analyzed the transformation of successive Canadian frontiers from socially disorganized settlements into organized societies. He then conducted research on how economic change in Canada resulted in inequality as reflected in patterns of residential segregation. His books include *The Canadian Manufacturers Association* (1939), *The Social Development of Canada* (1942), *Church and Sect in Canada* (1948), *Movements of Political Protest in Canada* (1959), *The Developing Canadian Community* (1962), *The Suburban Society* (1966), *Canadian Society in Historical Perspective* (1976) and *The New Urban Poor* (1978).

Clark served as president of the Canadian Political Science Association, honorary president of the Canadian Sociology and Anthropology Association and president of the Royal Society of Canada. He was awarded the J.B. Tyrell Historical Medal, became a foreign honorary member of the American Academy of Arts and Sciences and an Officer of the Order of Canada, and received honorary degrees from half a dozen Canadian universities.

In 1999, Clark's son, William Edmund (Ed) Clark, endowed the S.D. Clark Chair in Sociology at the University of Toronto in honour of his father.

Racism, Islamophobia, Antisemitism and the Future of Canadian Society

PROCEEDINGS OF THE FIFTH
S.D. CLARK SYMPOSIUM
ON THE FUTURE OF CANADIAN SOCIETY

EDITED BY
Robert Brym

Rock's Mills Press
Oakville, Ontario
2020

PUBLISHED BY

ROCK'S MILLS PRESS
www.rocksmillspress.com

Cover Photo: "Fight with Words"/Wildpixel/iStock.
Frontispiece photo: Courtesy Ed Clark.

For information, contact customer.service@rocksmillspress.com.

Contents

List of Figures

Racism, Islamophobia,
Antisemitism and the Future
of Canadian Society

CHAPTER ONE

Racism, Islamophobia, Antisemitism and the Future of Canadian Society[1]

Robert Brym

Earth continues to travel in a slightly elliptical orbit around the sun, but some years ago the world started veering to the right. In the United States, Brazil, Poland, Hungary and other countries, so-called "populist" governments came to power—and even where they didn't, they gained strength.

Populists in Western countries tend to be pro-capitalist, authoritarian and anti-immigration. They favour a society that is predominantly White and Christian. They prefer governments that concentrate power in the hands of one man yet refrain from using that power to provide citizens with comprehensive health, welfare and educational services. Instead, they prefer to leave such matters to privately-owned businesses that are owned or controlled by their ardent supporters. Populist leaders typically enjoy a privileged background. Nonetheless, they call their opponents "elites," by which they mean urban, relatively well-educated individuals who are presumably out of touch with the needs and demands of "the people," whom they claim to represent.

The rise of populism stretches the sociological imagination, but not because those who have been elected to high office tend to be privileged White male Christians. That pattern has been the norm since the first so-called mass democratic election was held in 1828, when a majority of White male property owners were permitted to vote for the US President. What is surprising is that so many people support populist leaders today.

Which people? According to surveys conducted in many countries, supporters of populist parties and movements tend to be individuals who feel threatened culturally and/or economically by the magnitude and speed with which capital and people now move across borders (Brym 2016; Inglehart and Norris 2017).

For more than four decades, particularly in North America,

<hr />

1. I thank Abdie Kazemipur and Rhonda Lenton for comments on a draft.

capital flowed to foreign low-wage jurisdictions, undermining manufacturing industries and increasing the proportion of low-quality jobs here (Tal 2019). At the same time, an aging population and a declining total fertility rate necessitated more immigration. Economists and demographers tell us that without immigration, Canada's population would start to shrink in 2034 (Conference Board of Canada 2018). Partly because governments provide inadequate opportunities for upgrading the skills and credentials of downwardly mobile workers and immigrants, the downwardly mobile, egged on by populist leaders, become angry, while immigrants become targets of their anger.

In 2017, Canada's leading public opinion pollster, Michael Adams, comforted us with data showing that it couldn't happen here. "We've had our flings with polarizing populists," he wrote, "but when the buzz wears off, we always seem to muddle our way back to the middle" (Adams 2017: 153). Yet, just one year later, the *Coalition Avenir Québec* took power in *la belle province* and Doug Ford became Premier of Ontario. Today, more than six of ten Canadians live under provincial regimes that espouse populist sentiments; nearly one of four Canadians reside in a province that has banned the display of religious symbols by educators, police officers and legal personnel employed by the province; nearly two of three Canadians believe "the government should prioritize limiting immigration levels because the country might be reaching a limit in its ability to integrate them;" and nearly four of ten believe that "immigration is a threat to white Canadians" (Abedi 2019; Wright 2019).

In 1967, the CBC invited the Reverend Martin Luther King to deliver the prestigious Massey Lectures. He flattered us in his inimitable voice:

> Deep in our history of struggle for freedom Canada was the North Star. The Negro slave ... knew that far to the north a land existed where a fugitive slave, if he survived the horrors of the journey, could find freedom. The legendary underground railroad started in the south and ended in Canada.... Our spirituals, now so widely admired around the world, were often codes. We sang of "heaven" that awaited us, and the slave masters listened in innocence, not realizing that we were not speaking of the hereafter. Heaven was the

word for Canada and the Negro sang of the hope that his escape on the underground railroad would carry him there. One of our spirituals, "Follow the Drinking Gourd," in its disguised lyrics contained directions for escape. The gourd was the big dipper, and the North Star to which its handle pointed gave the celestial map that directed the flight to the Canadian border (King 1967: 1).

King was a better guest than an historian of Canada. After the American Civil War, the practice of allowing Black settlement in Canada was reversed. Most immigration applications by Black people were rejected. Although freed from slavery in 1834, Blacks living in Canada were subjected to a high level of residential and occupational segregation, not to mention daily reminders that equality was not really intended for them. Immigration regulations were finally liberalized in the 1960s, but new laws and much trumpeting of multiculturalism since the early 1970s have not erased Black-White gaps either in the country's child welfare, educational and criminal justice systems or in the labour market. In their contribution to this volume, Akwasi Owusu-Bempah and Carl E. James focus on the criminal justice system, but they also show how all the settings just listed feed into one another to keep Black-White gaps in place. They thus paint a markedly less rosy picture than those to which we may be accustomed, but a picture that has the virtue of realism.

In his chapter on Islamophobia, Abdolmohammad Kazemipur finds that Canada really has been different from the United States and France in some respects. Notably, until recently, our parliamentary debates and public institutions tended to regard Muslim issues as a foreign concern of little significance domestically. However, public discourse shifted in the direction of the US/France model in the wake of al-Qaeda's 2001 attacks on centres of US power, two foiled terrorist attacks on Canadian soil in 2014, the impassioned debate on immigration that surfaced during the 2015 federal election campaign and the hardening of anti-immigration and pro-assimilationist rhetoric in Quebec around the same time. The latter culminated in the election of the *Coalition Avenir Québec* in 2018 and, a year later, the passage of Bill 21, prohibiting the wearing of visible religious symbols such as hijabs in certain public professions.

Kazemipur also exposes an area in which Canadian-style Islamophobia flourishes almost unnoticed: the labour market. He relies on data from a unique Statistics Canada panel survey of 2000-01 immigrants covering the period 2003–15. After matching religious groups on occupational, age and gender composition, immigration category, level of education, visible-minority status and other potentially confounding variables, he finds that Muslims were the only religious group in Canada that had significantly lower annual income than Catholics, the country's plurality religious group. True, the income gap between Muslims and Catholics narrowed between 2003 and 2011. However, in 2015, it dropped back almost to the 2003 level. The timing suggests that the earlier-noted shift in Canadian discourse concerning Muslims resonated in the labour market, increasing discrimination against Muslims.

My slang thesaurus proves that only one group rivals Blacks for terms of opprobrium routinely thrown in their face: Jews, the subject of Morton Weinfeld's chapter (Green 1986: 112–3). (My slang thesaurus was published in 1986. Muslims, who didn't even rate an entry back then, may have since caught up.)

The picture sketched by Weinfeld is one of Jews entering the mainstream of Canadian society in the 1960s after a century or so of exclusion. Quebec remains retrograde in some respects; attitudinal measures of anti-Jewish sentiment are typically twice as high in Quebec as in the rest of Canada, although in terms of educational and occupational attainment, Jews in Montreal are as much a part of the mainstream as are their co-religionists in Toronto.

As early as the mid-1980s, it was legitimate for some students of the subject to argue that antisemitism was dying out, hanging on only in withering right-wing circles and among some Eastern European communists who continued to find it politically useful (Hertzberg 1983). The turn to populism gave the lie to such optimism, as Weinfeld documents. Some indicators apparently exaggerate the increased frequency of antisemitic acts in Canada. However, fairly reliable data from police reports indicate a recent uptick in the frequency of hate crimes against Jews. Between 2006 and 2017, an annual average of 1,356 hate crimes was reported to the police. Jews were the victim of 15 percent of hate crimes, second only to Blacks at 20 percent. Since 2015, Muslims and Arabs/West Asians (mainly Iranians) have moved into first place (Brym 2019).

The authors of all three papers offer useful recommendations for dealing with anti-Black racism, Islamophobia and antisemitism—some legislative and regulatory, others social and political. Some of these recommendations are relevant to all minority ethnic and racial groups that face prejudice and discrimination. That is unsurprising since, as Neda Maghbouleh rightly observes in her concluding remarks, anti-Black racism, Islamophobia and antisemitism thrive in the same polluted waters; thus, she notes, cross-group solidarity in the face of swelling hate can itself be a powerful force for change.

At the same time, it serves no useful purpose to paper over differences that stand in the way of inter-group solidarity. To borrow an example that Weinfeld touches on, it seems that many if not most Muslims deny the legitimacy of the State of Israel, while most Jews regard attempts to delegitimize it as a form of antisemitism. In 1947, after the Holocaust, the United Nations passed resolution 181, partitioning British Mandatory Palestine into Arab and Jewish states; the resolution used the term "Jewish state" 30 times. Many Jews ask why now, more than seven decades later, theirs is the world's only state whose very existence is being challenged.[2] On the other hand, most Muslims are exasperated and angry with Israel's refusal to agree to the creation of a Palestinian state based on borders that existed before Israel's occupation of the West Bank and Gaza in 1967; many reject the legitimacy of any Jewish state in the region (Fatah 2009). In light of such differences, the existence of little more than a narrow strip of common ground between Muslims and Jews on this issue plays to the advantage of their joint enemies. It seems to me that the broadening of that strip is a tough but necessary task in the struggle against hate.

2. Forty-three countries have an official state religion. The most common state religion is Islam (27 countries), followed by Christianity (13 countries), Buddhism (two countries) and Judaism (one country). See Pew Research Center (2017).

References

Abedi, M. 2019. 37% in Ipsos poll say immigration is a "threat" to white Canadians—what's the threat? *Global News*, 23 May. https://bit.ly/336Vu8t.

Adams, M. 2017. *Could it Happen Here? Canada in the Age of Trump and Brexit*. Toronto: Simon and Schuster Canada.

Brym, R. 2016. After postmaterialism: an essay on China, Russia and the United States. *Canadian Journal of Sociology* 41(2): 195–211.

Brym, R. 2019. Antisemitic and anti-Israel actions and attitudes in Canada and internationally: a research agenda. *Patterns of Prejudice* 53(4): 407–20.

Conference Board of Canada. 2018. Imagining Canada's economy without immigration. https://bit.ly/2WnHswi.

Fatah. 2009. Full text of Fatah political program after it was ratified by Fatah conference. http://mideastweb.org/fatah_program_2009.htm.

Green, J. 1986. *The Slang Thesaurus*. London: Penguin.

Hertzberg, A. 1983. Is anti-Semitism dying out? *New York Review of Books* 40(12): 52–7.

Inglehart, R. and Norris, P. 2017. Trump and the populist authoritarian parties: the silent revolution in reverse. *Perspectives on Politics* 15(2): 443–54.

King, M.L. 1967. *Conscience for Change*. Toronto: CBC Learning Systems.

Pew Research Center. 2017. Many countries favor specific religions, officially or unofficially. https://pewrsr.ch/2EcanOX.

Tal, B. 2019. Lower job quality curbing income growth. *CIBC Economics*, 4 July. https://bit.ly/2ovSKSW.

Wright, T. 2019. Majority of Canadians think immigration should be limited: poll. *Global News*, 16 June. https://bit.ly/2q1CGZo.

CHAPTER TWO

Islamophobia in Canada between Populism and Political Correctness

Abdolmohammad Kazemipur

Introduction

The term "Islamophobia" surfaced in the late 1980s and was popularized in the mid-1990s by the publication of *Islamophobia: A Challenge for Us All*, the now-famous report of a British think tank. The report defines Islamophobia as "dread or hatred of Islam—and, therefore, ... fear and dislike of all or most Muslims" (Runnymede Trust 1997:1). Over the next two decades, more elaborate definitions of Islamophobia were proposed, but their common denominator comprises two elements: (1) a double standard in the view and treatment of Muslims; and (2) justification of the double standard by gross generalizations about what Muslims think and how they behave, that is, by generalizing the views of a minority of Muslims to all Muslims or generalizing the official views of Muslim-majority countries to their entire populations (Heyder and Eisentraut 2016).

The Runnymede report argued that dread and hatred of Muslims escalated in the 1970s, coinciding with the rise of political Islam or "Islamism" in the Middle East and, in particular, Iran's 1979 "Islamic Revolution." It was reinforced by a series of political developments, including the resistance of Jihadi groups to the Soviet invasion of Afghanistan, the assassination of Anwar Sadat in Egypt, the rise of Hezbollah in Lebanon, the formation of Islamist organizations in Palestine, the Salman Rushdie affair in the UK, the terrorist attacks of September 11, 2001, in the United States and subsequent attacks in Europe. Each of these events also facilitated the rise of right-wing "populist" politicians and political parties with anti-Muslim platforms. On the 20th anniversary of its report, the Runnymede Trust published a new volume, the title of which rang true: *Islamophobia: Still a Challenge for Us All* (Runnymede Trust 2017).

Notwithstanding the recency of the term "Islamophobia," anti-Muslim sentiment long predates the first report (Runnymede

Trust 1997:1). Its history can be traced back to the first decades after the rise of Islam in the early 7th century, when Muhammad's successors consolidated their power in the Arabian peninsula and began expanding outward, bringing them into contact with Europe. For nearly ten centuries thereafter, Europeans had first-hand encounters with Muslims—often military confrontations—in the Balkans, the Iberian peninsula, and the territory of what are today France and Austria. These clashes carved in the European psyche a spectre of Muslims as invaders and conquerors.

Fear of Muslims eventually found its way into contemporary Islamophobia. The most articulate statement of this linkage is found in the work of Samuel Huntington (1996; 2005), who saw the problematic relationship between Muslims and non-Muslims at global and local levels as the manifestation of a broad civilizational conflict, and Bernard Lewis (1987; 1991; 2000; 2001; 2002), who cited the historical resentment of Muslims toward the West as the source of today's conflictual relationship.

Where does Canada stand in this picture? So far as the treatment of minorities is concerned, Canada has long been considered—by its population, its government and non-Canadians—as an exception to global trends. The country has often been viewed as a bastion of tolerance, accommodation and fairness, in a world of rising intolerance, racism, exclusion, extremism and radicalism. Much evidence support the notion of "Canadian exceptionalism" (Banting and Kymlicka 2004; Environics 2019). To what extent can this claim be applied to Canadians' treatment of Muslims, particularly post-9/11?

Available information leads to a contradictory image. On the one hand, Muslims' satisfaction with life in Canada is significantly higher than their satisfaction with life in other western countries, rising even higher between 2006 and 2016 (Environics 2016). On the other hand, data show that, between 2014 and 2016, while the overall number of hate crimes declined in Canada, the incidence of hate crimes against Muslims and Arabs has been consistently rising (CBC 2016). Before the 2019 Christchurch mosque shooting in New Zealand, which left 51 Muslims dead and 49 injured, Canada was the only western country in which a mosque shooting had taken place (in 2017 in Quebec City, with six dead and nineteen injured). What does this conflicting information tell us about the state of Muslims in Canadian society and the seriousness of the problem of Islamophobia in this country?

Canada's brief encounter with Islam and Muslims

Canada's history of encounters with Islam and Muslims is an extremely short one compared to those of other western countries in Europe and North America.

For Europe, this history dates as far back as the 8th century, when Arab Muslims began their European advance. It brought Muslims face to face with Europeans in today's France, Spain and Austria. The encounter of Muslims with France was relatively short-lived because the advancing Muslim army was stopped, defeated and pushed back (at Poitiers in 732). Despite its brevity, the encounter was sufficient to imprint a nearly permanent fear of Muslims in the French psyche. After the defeat, the Muslims withdrew and settled in their previously conquered Iberian territories, a settlement that lasted from 731 to 1492 and created perhaps the most fruitful episode in the history of the Muslim-Europe encounter. Most historians consider this period a golden era of artistic, literary and intellectual vibrancy and of inter-religious tolerance and peaceful coexistence best symbolized by the combined Mosque-Cathedral of Córdoba (*Mezquita-Catedral de Córdoba*). However, some historians view Muslim Spain as just another example of Muslim tyranny (see Fernandez-Morera 2016). This period came to an end in 1492 when Spain was reconquered by Christian forces, but it permanently embedded Islam and Muslims in the Spanish psyche.

While the Spaniards were pushing Muslims out of Iberia and back to North Africa, a new Muslim army consisting of Ottoman Turks was advancing in the southeastern corner of Europe. Beginning in the middle of the 14th century, the Ottomans, with their centre of power in Constantinople (today's Istanbul), launched a series of wars against various European kingdoms and annexed large parts of Europe, including almost all of the Balkans, parts of Greece and stretching as far as the gates of Vienna. Perhaps the most symbolically important developments in the history of this violent encounter were the two unsuccessful sieges of Vienna in 1529 and 1683. They signaled the start of a decline that ended with the collapse of the Ottoman Empire during World War I. These encounters made Islam and Muslims an almost permanent element in the identity debates that surfaced in Europe throughout its medieval and modern history, but particularly so in recent decades.

The American encounter with Muslims was more recent, dating from the late 18th century. Thanks to their connection to Europe, the Founding Fathers borrowed European ideas about Islam and Muslims. However, in the course of transferring those ideas, they switched mainstream anti-Muslim and the minority pro-Muslim views (Spellberg 2013). Many influential figures in American history—Thomas Jefferson, John Adams, John Leland and others—argued vehemently in favour of equal civil rights for Muslims, including freedom of religion, the right to vote and the right to hold public office, even that of president. Remarkably, most of those who argued in favour of Muslims' civil rights had strong negative views toward Islam itself. It is astounding that they managed to separate their views on Islam from their position on the rights of Muslims as citizens—a distinction that was largely eclipsed in the post-9/11 environment. Moreover, their fight for the civil rights of Muslims took place although they were unaware of any Muslims living in the United States. This means that their arguments were driven, not by the pressures of a constituency that they had to satisfy, but by principle and the image of hypothetical Muslim citizens. Antipathy toward Muslims surfaced in the mid-19th century debate on Mormons. Many Americans felt that Mormonism was "Mahommedanism Yankeeized" (Wright 2016:210).

In contrast to Europe and the United States, Canada's encounter with Islam and Muslims is very recent. Individual Muslims have been in Canada for more than a century, but in such small numbers and with such little incident that their presence prompted no significant discussions (Selby 2018). Even the involvement of the Canadian government in the escape of six American diplomats after the American embassy in Tehran was taken over in November 1979 did not translate into the kind of negative popular sentiment towards Muslims that took shape in the United States. Canada's reputation as a participant in international peace-keeping missions, along with the absence of a colonial history in the Muslim world, contributed to making Islam and Muslims a non-issue in Canada.

The first sign of Canada's serious engagement with Muslims appeared in the mid-1990s. Lacking historical data on the degree of public sensitivity toward Islam and Muslims, I turned to parliamentary debate as an indicator of this sentiment. Figure 2.1 reports the frequency with which Muslims and/or Islam have been mentioned in Canadian parliamentary debates since the mid-1990s. The data show an initial surge in 1994, a second peak after 9/11, and a significant increase in the years 2013–17, culminating in the lead-up to the country's 2015 federal election.

The content of parliamentary discussion was also transformed. Figure 2.2 presents two word clouds, one for the period before pre-9/11, the other for the period after 9/11. They portray the frequency of words spoken in parliamentary debate concerning Islam and Muslims. The size of words is a function of the frequency of their use. As illustrated in Figure 2.2, discussions in parliament about Islam and Muslims have had a strong global focus; domestically, they have been a non-issue. For example, the 1995 debate on Muslims concerned almost exclusively the civil war between Christian Serbs and Muslim Bosnians in the former Yugoslavia. In that conflict, Canada (like the United States and several other western countries) supported the Bosnians. However, support did not translate into a discussion of Muslims in Canada, partly because the conflict was overseas. In addition, Bosnians were careful to portray themselves as ethnically Muslim and *not* to portray their conflict with Serbians as a Muslim-Christian issue. The west sided with Bosnians not as Muslims but as a population subjected to a brutal act of ethnic cleansing.

The 9/11 attack intensified discussion of Islam and Muslims in parliament and changed the content of those discussions. Now, the words Islam, religion, Arab, and terrorism were frequently used in parliamentarians' daily vocabulary. In 2014, the discovery of several terrorist plots and the execution of two acts of terrorism created fertile ground for open and critical discussion of Muslims, increased vandalization of mosques and Islamic centres and the 2017 mosque shooting in Quebec City. In 2014–15, the place of Muslims in the Canadian psyche shifted, and a surge of debate on Muslims in Canada was evident in parliament.

Figure 2.1   Frequency of references to Islam/Muslims in Canadian parliamentary debate, 1994-2016

Figure 2.2   The changing content of Canadian parliamentary debate
on Islam/Muslims, pre- and post-9/11

After 2013, the tone of Canadian debate on Muslims became more similar to debate in other western countries, particularly France and the United States. With the emergence of the Syrian and, later, North African refugee crisis, anti-Muslim sentiment was expressed more frequently and openly in the broader society, particularly in Quebec. In fact, the outcome of the 2015 federal election was largely decided by the position of different parties on Muslim issues. Of particular significance was the noticeable loss of support for the New Democratic Party in Quebec as a result of the party's opposition to *laïcité* (complete separation of state and religion to the point of prohibiting state employees from wearing religious garb or symbols).

The brevity of Canadians' encounter with Muslims has pluses and minuses. On the positive side, the encounter lacks the dead weight of historical confrontation, conflict, violence and intolerance. The downside is the absence of a deep and meaningful dialogue with and about Muslims, leaving the Canadian public and its government vulnerable to imported discourses developed in contexts that bear little resemblance to Canadian realities. The fact that the perpetrator of the 2017 Quebec City mosque shooting was inspired by Donald Trump's anti-Muslim rhetoric says much about the danger of such imports. This minus side of Canadians' brief encounter with Muslims makes the task of developing an empirically grounded, authentically Canadian dialogue on Muslims all the more urgent. To that end, I next survey the conceptual landscape in research on Islam, Muslims and Islamophobia before turning to Canadian data on this subject.

The conceptual landscape

Islamophobia is an under-theorized concept, especially in countries like Canada where this field of research is a recent arrival. Figure 2.3 reports a count of all social scientific journal articles published between 1964 and 2018 in which Islam and/or Muslims are at least mentioned in connection with Canada. The trend line illustrates gradually rising interest beginning in the 1990s, with large spikes in 2001 (after 9/11) and 2014. Until the 21st century, the frequency was low. Moreover, even into the 21st century, most academic articles relied on qualitative data from interview-based research and content analysis of political and media discourse. Large-scale empirical studies of Muslims' socio-economic experience are rare, partly due to weak appetite in the Canadian research community for quantitative analysis, partly due to the unavailability of reliable large-scale quantitative data. For example, in the Canadian census, only the religion question is asked every decade; all other questions are asked at five-year intervals.

Figure 2.3   Number of academic journal articles at least mentioning Islam/Muslims and Canada, 1964-2018

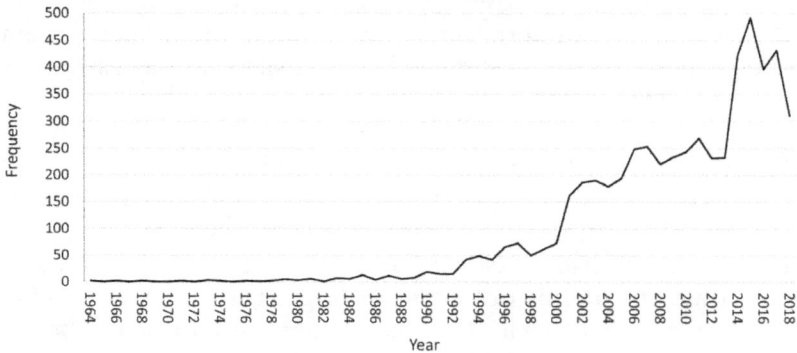

By contrast, European and, to a lesser extent, American research exhibits a deeper engagement with Islamophobia. Themes have emerged in this body of work that can prove useful to Canadian researchers. In what follows, I list and briefly discuss these themes, allowing me to elicit ideas that inform my subsequent data analysis.

Islamophobia vs Muslimophobia

The events of 9/11 produced a surge of Western interest in Muslims, as evidenced by a proliferation of academic positions, courses and programs focusing on Islamic history, theology and jurisprudence.

In part, this surge of interest was intended to overcome the paucity of empirical research on Muslim populations. However, it was also fed by the misleading assumption—a residue of Orientalism—that the conduct of Muslims is determined exclusively by Islam. This line of thinking allows quotations from the Qur'an to be "mobilized as an 'explanation' for the features and dispositions of 'the Muslims', independently of the actual roles that religiousness plays for each individual and what Muslim identity may mean individually, subjectively and contextually in each case, and independently of whether those concerned even consider themselves Muslims" (Müller-Uri and Opratko 2016:125).

With increasing awareness of the multiplicity of interpretations of Islam, and growth in the body of empirical research on Muslim populations, the distinction between the study of Islam and the study of Muslims has now become more apparent in the academic community. Nonetheless, the field still struggles with deciding between Islamophobia and Muslimophobia. These concepts are distinct. The former focuses on the content of a religion, the latter on the conduct of its followers, thus allowing one to have reservations about one without harbouring misgivings about the other. In practice, however, the two concepts overlap considerably. A German study has thus found a strong correlation between resentment against Islam and prejudice against Muslims, indicating that the former easily slips into the latter (Unal 2016)

Prejudice vs critique

A second area of disagreement concerns the most effective research strategies for distinguishing Islamophobia as a type of social prejudice from criticism of Islam/Muslims as an attitude (Heyder and Eisentraut 2016). This distinction is of great importance because, while the former could lead to unfair treatment of Muslims, the latter could be used to promote reform in Muslim communities. This is a distinction that is often missed in heated political debate on Islam/Muslims, both by extreme right-wing populists and extreme advocates of political correctness. Ignoring this distinction reduces a multi-dimensional problem to a single, oversimplified dimension.

A Canadian example of this predicament concerns a British Columbia court decision against polygamy in 2011. While discussion of this decision revolved largely around certain Mormon communities in British Columbia, the issue of polygamy among Muslims was also present. The argument of two academic expert witnesses in this case, who disagreed with the court's ruling, was as follows: "commitment to multicultural toleration entails taking seriously the claims of women within illiberal minority groups, acknowledging that they are capable of meaningfully choosing to commit themselves to a way of life beyond the mainstream" (Bennion and Joffe 2016:14). This position, while arising from concern for the protection of minority rights, could easily suppress efforts by Muslim men and women to reform the practice of polygamy in Muslim communities. In my view, a better-informed position would oppose prejudice against Muslims but allows critiques of Muslims as a way of keeping alive the prospect of reform in Muslim communities.

Thinking, talking and acting

Should one look for Islamophobia in prejudiced attitudes or discriminatory behaviour—or, to use another popular set of distinctions, in "the holding of derogatory social attitudes or cognitive beliefs, the expression of negative affect, [or] the display of hostile or discriminatory behavior toward members of a group on account of their membership [in] that group" (Brown 1995:8)? Such distinctions find little echo in research on Muslims. Most Islamophobia research investigates prejudicial attitudes, with a sharp focus on the content of media products and political discourse. Little effort has been expended on studying anti-Muslim discriminatory practices. This bias may be due partly to the fact that media performances and speeches are more easily observed than are behavioural practices. Moreover, the former are more easily analyzed qualitatively while the latter typically require quantitative analysis. In any case, the bias is unfortunate because anti-Muslim discriminatory behaviour is probably more consequential in terms of its effect on the lives of Muslims.

Islamophobia vs other targets of prejudice and discrimination

An issue that needs to feature more prominently in the field concerns the extent to which the study of Islamophobia requires unique conceptualization. At the one extreme are those who contend that Islamophobia is just the most recent manifestation of racism and anti-minority sentiment, belonging in the same family as antisemitism, anti-Black racism and so on. From this point of view, Islamophobia can be adequately explained using the same conceptual resources as employed in earlier research (for more, see Aschauer 2016).

An offshoot of this viewpoint concerns similarities and dissimilarities between Islamophobia and antisemitism. Here again, opinions differ on whether we are dealing with distinct phenomena. Some scholars argue against linking the two, even considering it "positively dangerous" to compare antisemitism and Islamophobia, perhaps fearing that doing so might lead to "downplaying antisemitism and exaggerating Islamophobia" (Cesarani 2011:8). Others regard the two phenomena as closely intertwined—so much so that, "because anti-Semitism is taboo in Germany, and because anti-Semites cannot openly utter anti-Semitic statements any more, Islamophobia may have become an outlet for hidden or latent anti-Semitism" (quoted in Hafez 2016:20).

Other reasons exist for arguing that, while there are commonalities among Islamophobia, anti-Black racism and antisemitism, the reduction of one to another may not be justified. For instance, one study shows that a rightist political orientation has a significant positive effect on anti-Muslim and anti-Islam sentiment but not on antisemitic prejudice. In addition, racism explains antisemitic prejudice better than it explains anti-Muslim and anti-Islam prejudice (Unal (2016:47-48). Such findings suggest that the issue of the relationship between Islamophobia and antisemitism is far from straightforward, may be context-dependent and should not be assumed.

The uniqueness of Islamophobia does not receive the same kind of attention that phobias against other ethnic, racial and religious groups receive for reasons that have been enumerated as follows:

> The first is the conceptualization of racism that assumes that the protections afforded to racial minorities conventionally conceived as involuntarily constituted should not be extended to Muslims because theirs is a religious identity that is voluntarily chosen. The second is that the way that religion per se is frowned upon by the contemporary intelligentsia invites the ridiculing of Muslims as being salutary for intellectual debate and not, therefore, an issue of discrimination. Third, while ethnic identities are welcomed in the public space, there is much more unease about religious minorities. Finally, some find it difficult to sympathize with a minority that is perceived to be disloyal or associated with terrorism, a view that leads to a perception of Muslims as a threat rather than as a disadvantaged minority, subject to increasingly pernicious discourses of racialization (Meer and Modood 2009: 335).

Historical interpretations in circulation in the West about Muslims and Jews contribute to this state of affairs: for the former, a history of seeking dominance, for the latter, mostly a history of suffering. These interpretations have weighed against the crystallization of sympathy for Muslims. Some recent historical scholarship contributes to this difficulty by highlighting negative Muslim-Western encounters—a practice which misses the point that anti-Muslim, anti-Jewish and anti-Black sentiment all "have a connected history that is rooted in the formative period of European modernity," in which "the formation of homogenous Christian nations ... was achieved through the 'exclusion' of Jews and Moors" (quoted in Hafez 2016:21).

Against the background I have sketched, it seems evident that the reduction of one type of racism and discrimination to another needs to be established empirically, rather than assumed *a priori*. As the authors of one study of the subject insist, "if we want to understand individual differences in attitudes toward Islam and Muslims, we cannot rely on general out-group attitudes, but we need to take into account cognitions and emotions that are specific for Muslims and Islam. In a similar vein, to understand attitudes toward Jews and Judaism, we should look at cognitions and emotions targeted specifically [at them]" (Noll and Dekker 2016:64).

Violence vs everyday practices of exclusion

Brutal attacks on religious minorities in the west, such as the Quebec City and Christchurch, New Zealand, mosque shootings, the shooting of Jews in a Pittsburgh synagogue and the antisemitic rallies in Charlottesville, Virginia, create a high level of awareness about the presence of hateful sentiment in society. Influenced by the horrific nature of such events, Statistics Canada and other agencies have started monitoring and reporting hate-based attacks on various minorities. Such attacks are often assumed to indicate public sentiment toward minorities. However, the assumption is questionable.

Hate crimes are the acts of extremists. Outliers at the tail of a normal distribution, they are poor indicators of public sentiment in the middle of a normal curve. Consider the Pew Research Center's (2017) inter-group feeling thermometer, based on large representative samples of the American population. In 2014 and 2017, the warmest views of the American population were expressed toward Jews, warmer even than sentiments expressed toward Catholics and Protestants. Furthermore, warmth of feeling toward Jews increased from 2014 to 2017. The fact that hate crimes against Jews peaked during this period indicates the absence of a correlation between hate crimes and public sentiment. A similar argument may be made about attacks on Muslims in Canada and New Zealand, two countries with relatively low anti-Muslim sentiment as revealed by public opinion polls. The fact that nearly all observers—officials, academics and ordinary citizens—were surprised and expressed disgust and anger regarding these attacks indicates that the perpetrators were outliers.

A more controversial hypothesis concerns the possible existence of a positive correlation between support for political correctness and the likelihood of extreme events such as those mentioned earlier. Does the occurrence of extreme acts of violence in countries where they were least expected and that had few prior signs of overt Islamophobia and antisemitism compared to Europe suggest that they might be partly a consequence of the dominance of political correctness? One way for political correctness to give rise to violent extremism is that it puts a lid on relatively mild forms of hostility, such as verbal abuse. Extreme levels of political correctness may therefore allow hostilities to gain strength and momentum. If nothing else, this hypothesis implies that social scientists might profitably conceptualize political correctness as a variable in inter-group dynamics. The value of doing so should be assessed empirically, not on an ideological or cultural basis, allowing for a critical, empirically based, engagement with the concept of political correctness and undermining the current monopoly of its critique from a conservative and ethnocentric perspective.

Muslims in Canada's public institutions and the economy

Against the conceptual background I have sketched, let us now turn to a discussion of the state of Islamophobia in Canada. I focus on Muslimophobia as opposed to anti-Islam sentiment and examine everyday practices of exclusion as opposed to acts of extreme violence. I highlight discriminatory practices rather than prejudicial attitudes. Finally, I direct my attention to the treatment of Muslims by Canadian public institutions and in Canadian economy.

Government and public institutions

As noted earlier, many post-9/11 debates on Muslims in the West are informed by the assumption that the behaviour of Muslims is driven by Islam, so change in that behaviour must stem from a change in Muslims' relationship to their faith (see, for instance, Harris 2004). As common as this perception is, it does not adequately explain the experiences of Muslims.

A first step toward refining the understanding of Muslim realities is to separate the discussion of Muslims from a discussion of

Islam. To what extent has this distinction taken root in Canada? To answer this question, I rely on the discussion of Muslims in Canadian parliamentary debates, using the frequency of references to Islam versus Muslims. I surmise that the more frequent the reference to Muslims rather than Islam, the healthier the intellectual environment for discussing Muslim issues.

Figure 2.4, Figure 2.5 and Figure 2.6 report frequencies for France, the United States and Canada, respectively. We observe an important difference between Canada and the other two countries. In the United States, since about 2005, references to Islam have been consistently higher than references to Muslims. In Canada, the trend is the opposite, with the exception of 2013-15. For France, the two trendlines are higher than in Canada and they move in tandem. They switch places frequently, but toward the end of the period under consideration the frequency of mentions of Islam exceeds the frequency of mentions of Muslims. Based on these data, the atmosphere for Muslims seems healthier in the Canadian parliament than in the lower houses of France and the United States. Why, then, is the period 2013–15 anomalous in Canada?

The years 2013-15 witnessed several important developments that engendered the "Europeanization" of Canadian discussions of Muslims. First, the period culminated in the 2015 federal election, the outcome of which was to a large extent decided by the positions of the major political parties on Muslim-related issues. Second, anti-Muslim sentiment in Quebec hardened, resulting in a stronger emphasis on *laïcité* and the need to assimilate immigrants. Third, the federal government, then led by Stephen Harper's Conservatives, found the Quebec approach to immigrants and Muslims appealing and began adopting it.

Figure 2.4   Frequency of references to Islam/Muslims in French parliament, 1987-2017

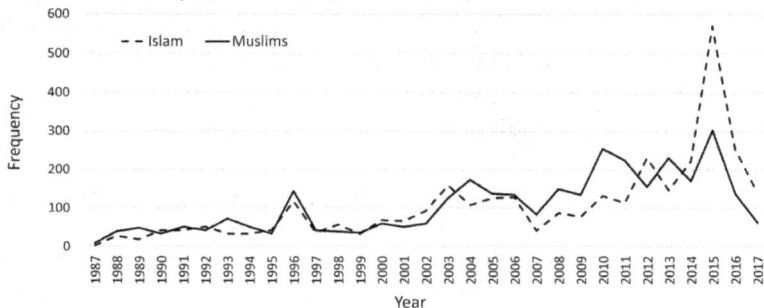

Source: Assemblée nationale (1987-2017).

Figure 2.5   Frequency of references to Islam/Muslims
in US congress, 1995-2017

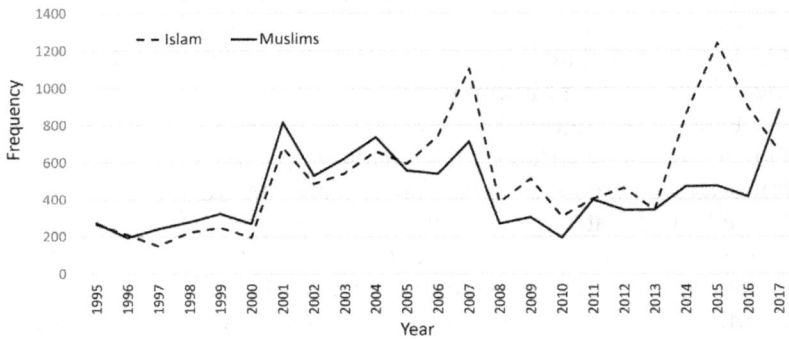

Source: United States Congress (1995-2017).

Figure 2.6   Frequency of references to Islam/Muslims
in Canadian parliament, 1995-2017

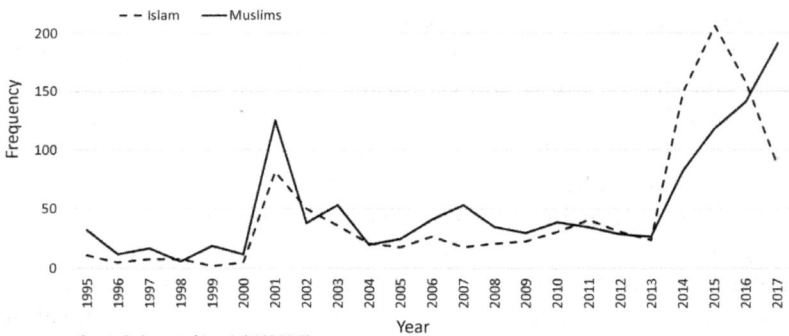

Source: Parliament of Canada (1995-2017).

The federal Conservatives were defeated in the 2015 and 2019 elections. However, the Quebec model became more deeply entrenched in Quebec, particularly with the passage of Bill C-21 in 2019. The new law prohibited the wearing of religious symbols by public servants, thus bringing Quebec close to adopting the policy of *laïcité* that originated in France. As such, Quebec stands out as the North American jurisdiction most strongly driven by Islamophobic sentiment.

Beside Quebec's government, the Canada's justice system and security apparatus are two institutions in which conspicuous anti-Muslim practices have been committed. In several high-profile cases, the rights of Muslims seem to have been visibly ignored, some with devastating consequences. They include the cases of Omar

Khadr, Mahar Arar, Hassan Diab and Rania El-Alloul, as well as a recent instance of racial and religious discrimination committed by the Canadian Security Intelligence Service (CSIS) against one of the agency's Muslim employees (Gatehouse 2020). Each of these cases involved discriminatory behaviour and/or abusive treatment by a public institution. What was the source of this problem?

To answer this question precisely, one must keep two things in mind. First, we need to establish whether the source of the wrongdoing resided in the institution's structure, mandate, culture or the discretion of the people who made key decisions in each case. Providing details for each case would take us too far afield, but my assessment is that in most if not all the cases just listed, institutional culture or the bias of people in key decision-making positions were at fault. In the cases involving CSIS, it seems that the culprit was an anti-Muslim institutional culture. Making this point is crucial when it comes to suggesting remedies. Depending on the identified source of the problem, the solution may be reform of an institution's mandate, rules and regulations; cultural sensitivity training for personnel; or a cultural awareness campaign in the broader society.

The second point to bear in mind in assessing the cases at hand is that, while wrongdoing by Canadian authorities was the main source of victimization in each case, the wrongdoings were eventually acknowledged by the institutions involved and unjust decisions were overturned. In some cases, compensation was paid. The institutions were able to self-correct or be corrected by other government bodies. This capacity may be read as an indication of the absence of built-in bias against Muslims in the structure or mandate of Canadian public institutions.

Muslimophobia and the Canadian economy

In contrast to the Canadian government and public institutions, the Canadian economy is the site of strong bias against Muslims. Evidence of this bias has been consistent at least since 2001. I reach this conclusion by examining the income trends and employment rate of immigrants who arrived in Canada between 1 October 2000 and 30 September 2001 for their first fifteen years in the country. They show that Muslims report the lowest employment rates and incomes compared to immigrants of all other religious backgrounds (for details, see Kazemipur and Evra 2018; Evra and Kazemipur 2019). Given that the same income and employment trends could have been caused by factors other than religion—such as immigration category (for example, they might have a preponderance of refugees rather than skilled workers), level of education, visible-minority status, access to social networks or occupational, age and gender composition—a more accurate assessment of the role of religion requires the effects of such variables to be controlled. Figure 2.7 reports the refined findings. The trendlines show the result of a multiple regression analysis—specifically, change in beta coefficients—for the impact of religious background on income at four-year intervals beginning in 2003 and ending in 2015.

In Figure 2.7, the baseline (or reference category) consists of Catholics, Canada's plurality religious group, represented by the horizontal dashed grey line. Between 2003 and 2011, all the other lines converge towards the baseline. This means that for Muslims and non-Muslims, and relative to Catholics, the negative impact of religious status on immigrants' income diminished. This must be considered a positive development insofar as it left more room for human capital factors to influence income, which is expected in a meritocratic job market and is in line with Canadian immigration policy.

Figure 2.7   The impact of religion on income, 2003-15, with controls (beta coefficients)

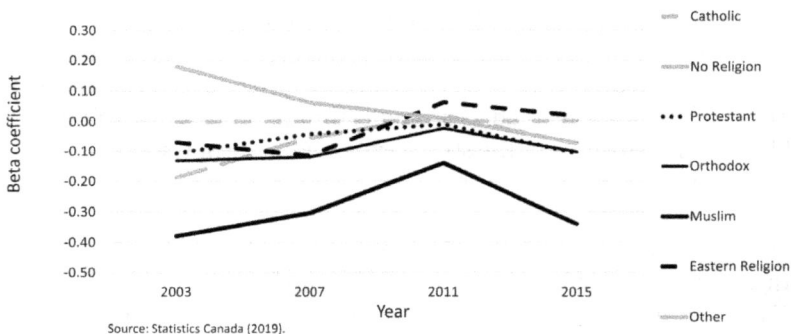

Source: Statistics Canada (2019).

However, Figure 2.7 illustrates a reversal of this trend between 2011 and 2015; the trendlines diverge from the baseline in 2011 and move downward. Despite the presence of a similar decline for all religious groups, the magnitude of the decline was not statistically significant for any of them at the .05 level—except for Muslims (represented by the solid black line at the bottom of Figure 2.7). In 2015, religion became significantly more influential in determining the income of Muslim immigrants alone. The fact that the beta coefficients report the impact of religion after controlling for other relevant variables indicates that the unique experience of Muslims cannot be attributed to such factors as education, immigration status, age, sex, occupation and so on.

Two things happened in 2015 that may have been responsible for the significant decline in Muslim income in that year. First, Trump's run for the US presidency began. The vitriol Trump poured on Muslims oozed into Canada, where three-quarters or more of television programming comes from the United States and Canadian news outlets cover every twist and turn of American presidential campaigns, especially those steeped in controversy. Simultaneously, the Canadian federal election campaign was in full swing, accompanied by a level of anti-Muslim rhetoric never before seen in this country, especially in Quebec. In the absence of plausible alternative explanations, it is not unreasonable to hypothesize that this atmosphere increased anti-Muslim discrimination in the Canadian job market and was responsible for the significant decline in Muslim income in 2015.

Research and policy implications

My analysis permits two conclusions. First, when it comes to the experience of Muslims and the occurrence of Islamophobia, a uniquely Canadian situation seems to exist. Second, the uniqueness of the Canadian situation seems to have dissipated somewhat in the 2010s.

My findings suggest the need for more quantitative, refined and frequent data collection on topics relevant to Islamophobia. For example, religious and ethnic self-definitions are more fluid and multiplex than Statistics Canada survey and census instruments allow, while the frequency of current data-generation practices by Statistics Canada cannot adequately capture developments in such a fast-changing field. Statistics Canada seems to have recognized this deficiency and has taken a step in the direction of fixing this problem by creating a consultative experts committee to advise on the status of data on immigrants and ethno-religious minorities.

The limitations of existing data notwithstanding, opportunities for policy intervention exist. First, public institutions always operate within a cultural environment, and in Canada this environment can benefit from cultural sensitivity training around the issue of religion. Such training may help ameliorate problems caused by biased institutional cultures and personality traits. Second, persistent anti-Muslim bias in the Canadian job market requires intervention in the form of legislation to protect disadvantaged groups, including

Muslim women and Black Muslims. Third, Islamophobia in public institutions and the job market might be mitigated by more face-to-face social interaction between Muslim and non-Muslim Canadians. Committing public resources to promoting such interaction could assist in the creation of a more hospitable and inclusive environment in Canada.

In the absence of such measures, the risk grows that Canadian discourse on Muslims will continue borrowing harmful ideas from societies that exhibit a high level of hostility toward Muslims. In the process, Canada might lose its distinctiveness and pioneering position in managing cultural, ethnic and religious diversity.

References

Aschauer, W. 2016. The multidimensional nature of Islamophobia: a mixed method approach to constructing the Attitudes Toward Muslims Scale (ATMS). *Islamophobia Studies Journal* 3(2): 131–58.

Assemblée nationale. 1987-2017. Recherche avancée des questions. http://www2.assemblee-nationale.fr/recherche/questions.

Banting, K. and Kymlicka, W. 2004. Canada, not America. *Prospect*. March: 1–10.

Bennion, J. and Joffe, L. F. 2016. Introduction. Pp. 3–24 in J. Bennion and L. F. Joffe, eds. *The Polygamy Question*. Logan, UT: Utah State University Press.

Brown, R. 1995. *Prejudice: Its Social Psychology*. London: Wiley-Blackwell.

CBC. 2016. Hate crimes were down in 2015 but police saw spike in incidents targeting Muslims. 17 March. https://www.cbc.ca/news/canada/toronto/hate-crimes-drop-toronto-police-muslim-spike-1.3496505.

Cesarani, D. 2011. Are Muslims the new Jews? Comparing Islamophobia and anti-Semitism in Britain and Europe. *YIISA Discussion Paper*. July 31. isgap.org/david-cesarani.

Environics Institute. 2016. Survey of Muslims in Canada 2016. https://www.environicsinstitute.org/projects/project-details/survey-of-muslims-in-canada-2016.

Environics Institute. 2019. Canadian public opinion about immigration and refugees. https://www.environicsinstitute.org/projects/project-details/canadian-public-opinion-on-immigration-and-refugees---focus-canada-spring-2019.

Evra, R. and Kazemipur, A. 2019. The role of social capital and ethnocultural characteristics in the employment income of immigrants over time. *Insights on Canadian Society*. Statistics Canada. https://www150.statcan.gc.ca/n1/pub/75-006-x/2019001/article/00009-eng.pdf.

Fernandez-Morera, D. 2016. *The Myth of the Andalusian Paradise: Muslims, Christians, and Jews under Islamic Rule in Medieval Spain*. Wilmington, Delaware: Intercollegiate Studies Institute.

Gatehouse, J. 2020. A "second class" spy: Muslim CSIS agent alleges discrimination, abuse: Lawsuit claims religious persecution by bosses, co-workers in "irretrievably hostile" workplace. CBC News, 21 January. https://www.cbc.ca/news/politics/csis-muslim-discrimination-lawsuit-1.5433654.

Hafez, F. 2016. Comparing anti-Semitism and Islamophobia: the state of the field. *Islamophobia Studies Journal* 3(2): 16–34.

Harris, S. 2004. *The End of Faith: Religion, Terror, and the Future of Reason*. New York: W. W. Norton & Company.

Heyder, A. and Eisentraut, M. 2016. Islamophobia and criticism of Islam: an empirical study of explanations using representative surveys from Germany. *Islamophobia Studies Journal* 3(2): 178–98.

Huntington, S. P. 1996. *The Clash of Civilizations and the Remaking of World Order*. New York: Simon & Schuster.

Huntington, S. P. 2005. *Who Are We?* New York: Simon & Schuster.

Kazemipur, A. and Evra, R. 2018. The first decade of the new life: the income trajectories of Canada's immigrants and refugees, 2001–2012. Paper presented at XIX ISA World Congress of Sociology, Toronto.

Lewis, B., ed. 1987. *Islam: From the Prophet Muhammad to the Capture of Constantinople*, vol. 1. New York: Oxford University Press.

Lewis, B. 1991. *The Political Language of Islam*. Chicago: University of Chicago Press.

Lewis, B. 2000. *The Middle East: 2000 Years of History from the Rise of Christianity to the Present Day*. London: Phoenix.

Lewis, B. 2001. The revolt of Islam. *The New Yorker*, 19 November. https://www.newyorker.com/magazine/2001/11/19/the-revolt-of-islam.

Lewis, B. 2002. *What Went Wrong? Western Impact and the Middle Eastern Response*. New York: Oxford University Press.

Meer, N. and Modood, T. 2009. Refutations of racism in the "Muslim question." *Patterns of Prejudice* 43(3–4): 335-54.

Müller-Uri, F. and Opratko, B. 2016. Islamophobia as anti-Muslim racism: racism without races, racism without racists. *Islamophobia Studies Journal* 3(2): 117–29.

Parliament of Canada. 1995-2017. Hansard Index. https://www.ourcommons.ca/DocumentViewer/en/35-1/house/hansard-index.

Pew Research Center. 2017. Americans Express Increasingly Warm Feelings Toward Religious Groups: Jews, Catholics continue to receive warmest ratings, atheists and Muslims move from cool to neutral. https://www.pewforum.org/2017/02/15/americans-express-increasingly-warm-feelings-toward-religious-groups/.

Runnymede Trust. 1997. *Islamophobia: A Challenge for Us All*. London: Runnymede Trust.

Runnymede Trust. 2017. *Islamophobia: Still A Challenge for Us All (A 20th-anniversary Report)*, F. Elahi and O. Khan, eds. London: Runnymede Trust.

Selby, J., Barras, A. and Beaman, L. G. 2018. Beyond accommodation: everyday narratives of Muslim Canadians. Vancouver: UBC Press.

Spellberg, D. A. 2013. *Thomas Jefferson's Quran: Islam and the Founders*. New York: Vintage.

Statistics Canada. 2019. Extended Longitudinal Survey of Immigrants to Canada (LSIC-IMDB). Statistics Canada Research Data Centre. https://crdcn.org/datasets/lsic-imdb-extended-longitudinal-survey-immigrants-canada.

Unal, F. 2016. Islamophobia & anti-Semitism: comparing the social psychological underpinnings of anti-Semitic and anti-Muslim beliefs in contemporary Germany. *Islamophobia Studies Journal* 3(2): 35-55.

United States Congress. 1995–2017. Congressional Record. https://www.congress.gov/congressional-record/2020/02/05/house-section.

van der Noll, J. and Dekker, H. 2016. Islamophobia and anti-Semitism: etiological similarities and differences among Dutch youth. *Islamophobia Studies Journal* 3(2): 56–70.

Wright, S. 2016. From Mohammedan despotism to creeping Sharia: cultural (re)productions of Islamophobia in the United States. *Islamophobia Studies Journal* 3(2): 201–13.

CHAPTER THREE

Race and Incarceration: The Experience of African Canadians[1]

Akwasi Owusu-Bempah and Carl E. James

Introduction

Canada is often praised as a tolerant nation that welcomes immigrants. In 2018, we admitted more than 300,000 immigrants from countries around the world (Statistics Canada 2020). As a result, Canadians report over 250 ethnic ancestries and speak more than 200 languages (Statistics Canada 2017a; 2017b). However, this diversity and positive reputation often hide the negative experiences of many racial minority groups in the country and whitewash Canada's deeply racist past. The experience of African Canadians with Canada's justice institutions is a case in point. Indeed, the overrepresentation of young Black men in the criminal justice system is increasingly acknowledged by scholars and policymakers as an important social issue. Despite a decline in the overall inmate population, the number of Black offenders confined in Canadian federal correctional institutions increased by 75 percent in the decade leading up to 2012. Whereas Black Canadians represent just 2.9 percent of the Canadian population, they account for 9.3 percent of the total federal prison population (Office of the Correctional Investigator, 2013a).

Over the past few decades, numerous task forces and commissions have drawn attention to social factors that increase involvement in crime and have identified evidence of systemic racial discrimination in child welfare, education and justice institutions that leads to incarceration. Yet the problem of Black over-incarceration persists. In this paper we argue that the problem of Black over-incarceration is rooted in Canada's racist and colonial history and is a symptom of the discrimination Black people continue to experience in Canadian society. Slavery and legalized segregation formed the basis for Black Canadians' initial relationship with the state and its people. The ideas and assumptions on which they were based shaped

1. An earlier version of this paper was prepared for an expert report submitted by Owusu-Bempah and James in the criminal trial of R v Morris, 2018 ONSC 5186.

the nature of social relations. As evidenced by public opinion polls, some of these beliefs and ideas are still entrenched in the minds of many Canadians—particularly those associating Black people with crime and violence.

Incarceration serves as a useful tool to deal with a population long deemed problematic. We note that the introduction of a novel initiative in Canadian sentencing may decrease the over-incarceration of African Canadians but argue that the situation will not markedly improve until we reckon with our history and provide for the full integration of African Canadians into the country's social, political and economic life. We begin by outlining the early experience of Black people in Canada. We next document Black peoples' contemporary experience with child welfare, education and employment, outlining how they influence criminalization. Finally, we examine the experience of Black men in the Canadian criminal justice system and criticize a proposed solution for mitigating Black over-incarceration.

Anti-Black racism in Canada

People of African descent have a long history of residing in Canada and have played an integral part in the formation of the nation. The first documented person of African descent in Canada, Mathieu Da Costa, served as a translator to French and Dutch explorers beginning in 1609 (Winks 1997). Black people were subsequently brought to Canada as slaves from the early 17th century until slavery was abolished in 1834. Many Blacks arrived in Canada, particularly Nova Scotia and Ontario, by means of the Underground Railroad as fugitive slaves from the United States (Maynard 2017; Winks 1997). Most of Ontario's Black settlements were in the south, especially in and around the Windsor, Chatham, London, St. Catharines and Hamilton areas. Others formed small groupings in Toronto and outside of Barrie, Owen Sound and Guelph. These concentrated Black communities served as a buffer against prejudice and discrimination from the White population. The historical record suggests that Black people in Canada were generally treated with hostility and disdain.

The fact that at least six of the first sixteen legislators of Upper Canada held slaves supports the view that early Canadian settlers viewed the Black population as property. As the institution of chattel slavery was predicated on the idea that slaves are not human beings, it is reasonable to suggest that the initial experience of Black people in Canada was one of second-class citizenship. Indeed, after slavery was abolished, Blacks experienced segregation, de jure and de facto, in education, employment, housing and other spheres of social life; legislation allowing segregated schools in Ontario remained on the books until 1964 (Henry and Tator 2005). These experiences served to put Canada's Black population at a severe economic and political disadvantage while simultaneously privileging White Canadians (Wortley and Owusu-Bempah 2011). This history also sets the stage for the experience of more recent Black immigrants by creating a framework of anti-Black racism that continues to express itself across various facets of Canadian society.

Canada, like many other Western nations, still shoulders the burden of colonialism. A key feature of the experience of Black Canadians has been racism and, concomitantly, discrimination, as evident in the erasure of the contributions Black people have made to this country (Morgan 2016). The participation of Black Canadians in military service, politics, education and entrepreneurship goes largely unmentioned in the media, is almost completely omitted from school curricula and thus contributes to the perpetuation of anti-Black racism. At the same time, the full extent of the discrimination experienced by Black people remains under-reported (Henry and Tator 2005; Cole 2020). Without a clear historical contextualization of Black disadvantage, the under-achievement of Black students, Blacks' over-representation among the unemployed and their increased presence in correctional facilities is easily explained by reference to stereotypical assumptions about the Black work ethic, the nature of Black families and Blacks' supposed innate propensity for crime and violence (James 2018; Owusu-Bempah 2017).

Canadian public opinion polls show that most Canadians continue to hold at least slightly racist opinions of Black community members, while 84 percent of Canadian Black people believe they are often or sometimes treated unfairly by other Canadians because of their race (Environics Institute 2019:35; Patriquin 2007). Various forms of racism have been extensively documented by scholars and acknowledged by government commissions and task forces for decades (Cole 2020). In Ontario, evidence of government concern dates from the 1980s and was evidenced most recently in the formation of the Anti-Racism Directorate and the Toronto Action Plan to Confront Anti-Black Racism in 2016. These and other initiatives show that Black people in Canada, regardless of place of birth or length of time in the country, continue to face challenges that influence their experience and life chances. Yet myriad initiatives, accompanying reports and lengthy lists of recommendations mean little if they have scant influence on the actions of key decision makers and the behaviour of ordinary Canadians.

To contextualize the experience of young Black men in the criminal justice system, we next outline the nature and extent of discrimination, marginalization and exclusion that they experience across various institutions and areas of social life in Ontario today. We begin by examining Black children in the youth and child welfare systems.

The experience of Black children and youth in the child welfare system

Racism and poverty are responsible for the disproportionate representation of Black Canadian children in Ontario's welfare system (Fallon et al. 2015). Although Black Canadians comprise only 8.5 percent of the population of Toronto, 40.8 percent of Black children are in care (Ontario Association of Children's Aid Societies 2016: 4).

Concerns about Black Canadians' experiences with Ontario's child welfare system have been raised for decades by service users, advocates, community partners and the media (Ontario Association of Children's Aid Societies 2016; Ontario Human Rights Commission 2018). These concerns revolve around increased levels of surveillance that target Black families and result from the widely held belief that Black families are unfit and pathological (Maynard 2017; Roberts, 2002). Moreover, service users report that Black children and youth are treated differently than White children and youth, experiencing more negative outcomes and less access to required services.

The social circumstances of Black Canadians play a key role in influencing their experience in this system. An analysis of data from Ontario's child welfare agencies found that Black children are more likely to be investigated than are White children, though little evidence suggests that race alone was responsible for race differences in cases that were substantiated. Black families are more likely to be transferred to ongoing services, and children from Black families are more likely to be placed in out-of-home care. Severe economic hardship, combined with assessments about the quality of the parent-child relationship, contributed substantially to the decision to put a child in care (King et al. 2017).

As with Indigenous peoples, assessments of parent-child relationships are based on White middle-class norms about family and parenting that are culturally biased against Black families. For example, the practice of extended families caring for children, common outside the Western world, may clash with Western notions of the nuclear family and ideas about who should have primary responsibility for raising children. These differences are compounded by the economic hardships facing many Black people in Toronto, which result in parents working long hours to support their families while children are left in the care of grandparents, aunts, uncles or siblings.

Given concern about Black overrepresentation in the child welfare system, the Children's Aid Society of Toronto held a series of community consultations with the city's Black communities a few years ago. Participants included parents who were involved with the organization, adults who were in care as children, social service staff, and members of organizations that partner with child welfare agencies (Children's Aid Society of Toronto 2015). A resounding theme of these consultations was the high degree of fear and mistrust of the system. Parents and caregivers said that they were not being "listened to" by service providers and that children in care were not being heard. While participants acknowledged the need for child protection services to keep children safe from abuse, they also stressed the need for improved transparency and a greater range of service options for Black families. Significantly, a widespread perception existed of collusion between the main institutional systems that support Black children—namely, child welfare, education, and criminal justice.

Overrepresentation of African Canadian children and youth in Ontario's child welfare system and their experience of discrimination in this system present several areas of concern. The removal of Black children from their parents disrupts Black families, thus weakening kinship ties that are important for the emotional and social development of children and youth (Owusu-Bempah and Howitt 1997). Because contact with the child welfare system is a predictor of later offending, disproportionate levels of contact with the system, combined with the absence of culturally appropriate practices, increase the criminogenic effect of care for African Canadians (Jonson-Reid and Barth 2000; Owusu-Bempah 2007; 2010). Furthermore, the high rate of contact with the system and the removal of Black children from their parents reinforce negative stereotypes about the fragility of Black families and further pathologize African Canadian communities.

In sum, experience with the child welfare system acts as a catalyst for criminal offending and is a burden disproportionately inflicted on Black Canadians. Their increased exposure to child welfare increases their chance of exposure to the criminal justice system. The failure of Ontario's education system to adequately address the needs of Black students also plays a role in increasing criminalization.

The experience of Black children and youth in education

The relationship between educational failure and criminalization is well established (Groot and van den Brink 2010; Lochner and Morett 2004). Poor academic performance, absence from school and failure to graduate all increase the likelihood of offending.

As is the case with child welfare, concerns about Black students' academic underachievement have been evident in Ontario for decades. In 1987, the Provincial Advisory Committee on Race and Ethnocultural Relations was formed following a provincial conference on race and ethnocultural relations. The Committee prepared a Working Paper in 1988 entitled "The Development of a Policy on Race and Ethnocultural Equity" (Ministry of Education 1988). Shortly thereafter, in the wake of the "Yonge Street Riot," NDP Premier Bob Rae commissioned Stephen Lewis to investigate the state of race relations in Ontario.

The 1992 Stephen Lewis Report highlighted a lack of progress in improving educational outcomes for Black students. Lewis outlined the concerns of Black students drawn from consultations held in the Toronto region. These concerns included lack of racial diversity among teachers, absence of Black people and Black history in the curriculum, tolerance of racist incidents in schools, harsher discipline of Black students, streaming of Black students into courses below their level of ability and discouragement of Black students from attending university. Similar findings by other government-sponsored initiatives led to the NDP's amendments to the Education Act in 1992. The amendments called on school boards to develop and implement anti-racism and ethnocultural equity policies that promote the identification and elimination of systemic inequities and barriers to equitable education for students and encourage equitable education practices for staff (James and Turner 2017).

The positive sentiment derived from these suggestions was short lived. Conservative leader Mike Harris campaigned on an anti-employment equity platform and a promise of increased discipline in schools. His party formed the government in 1995. In 2000, a Code of Conduct for Ontario schools was released, followed soon after by amendments to the Education Act granting legal force to the Code of Conduct. It gave principals and teachers more authority to suspend and expel students, making expulsions and suspensions mandatory for serious infractions and establishing a zero-tolerance policy for inappropriate behaviour. This approach was criticized for suspending students for minor incidents and for being especially harsh on Black students (Puxley 2007). In 2007, the Ontario Human Rights Commission and the Ministry of Education finalized a settlement to replace the zero-tolerance policy with a progressive discipline approach to dealing with inappropriate school behaviour. Despite seemingly positive changes to the Education Act, including the implementation of an Equity and Inclusive Education Strategy in 2009, Black students continue to face poor educational prospects.

The streaming of Black students into non-university-track programs in schools has been an ongoing concern for students, parents, educators, community activists and some politicians. Concern centres on the perception that the streaming of Black students into non-university-track programs results from the stereotype that Black people are less intelligent, less academically inclined and thus more suited to vocational or college-based programs than are White students (James 2012: 482–484). Thus, in the 2006–11 cohort study, 53 percent of Black students, 81 percent of White students and 80 percent of other racialized students were in the Academic program of study. Black students (39 percent) were more than twice as likely as White students (16 percent) and students from other racialized backgrounds (18 percent) to be enrolled in the Applied program. Black students were also three times as likely to be enrolled in the Essentials program (9 percent versus 3 percent of White and other racialized students) (James and Turner 2017: 30).

Suspension and expulsion rates are also an important indicator of academic success insofar as they reflect time spent outside the educational system, thus influencing student's attachment to school, peers, and teachers. Exclusion from school is widely recognized as a driver for wider social exclusion and is highly correlated with unemployment and involvement in crime. As the Director General of HM Prison Service in the UK noted: "The 13,000 young people excluded from school each year might as well be given a date by which to join the prison service some time later down the line" (Martin Narey, cited in McMurtry and Curling 2008: 56).

Suspensions and expulsions may be particularly detrimental if they are perceived by students to be unjust, which in the case of Black youth, they often are; Black students are often stereotyped as "troublemakers" and often subject to increased surveillance and school disciplinary action that align with this stereotype (James 2012: 480-82; Ruck and Wortley 2002: 190). In the 2006–11 TDSB cohort, Black students were more than twice as likely as White and other racialized students to have been suspended at least once during the academic year. Upon graduation, 42 percent of all Black students had been suspended at least once, compared with only 18 percent of White students and 18 percent of other racialized students. Similar disparities exist with respect to expulsions. The TDSB data show that of the 213 students who were expelled between 2011–12 and 2015–16, 48 percent were Black (James and Turner 2017: 36).

Finally, the data indicate that Black students' academic success, measured by graduation rates, is far below that of their peers. Among the 2006–11 cohort, 84 percent of White students had graduated from high school at the end of five years, compared to 87 percent of other racialized students. By contrast, just 69 percent of Black students had graduated from high school over the same five-year period. Likewise, Black students were twice as likely (11 percent) as White and other racialized students (both 5 percent) to be returning to high school the following year when they should have graduated and twice as likely to have dropped out (20 percent) compared to White (11 percent) and other racialized students (9 percent) (James and Turner 2017: 31).

The Roots of Youth Violence report asserts that anti-Black racism in schools, and zero-tolerance policies in particular, contributed heavily to the school-to-prison pipeline (McMurtry and Curling 2008). If Black students are not afforded the same opportunities for academic success as their peers, their life-chances suffer. Poor educational outcomes for Black students ultimately have a negative impact on their employment prospects and earning potential. These problems affect not only individual Black Canadians but their families and communities.

Black employment and poverty

Comparatively low academic attainment combined with structural and institutional forms of discrimination converge to produce inequalities in Canada's employment sector. Given the poor educational outcomes for Black students noted earlier, it is unsurprising that Black youth are particularly vulnerable to unemployment. In Toronto, the unemployment rate in 2014 for Black youth between the ages of 15 and 24 was 30 percent compared to 20 percent of youth from other racial backgrounds (CivicAction 2014).

A high rate of Black unemployment is not a new phenomenon. Evidence suggests that Black job seekers are excluded from the labour market in part due to the discriminatory actions of employers. In the early 1980s, one study examined the impact of race and foreignness (indicated by name or accent) on the likelihood of being offered a job. Black and White actors were sent to interviews with identical résumés but Black applicants experienced discrimination in one-quarter of job contacts, which could not have happened by chance alone (Henry and Ginzberg 1985).

Recent research has produced remarkably similar results. One researcher created four fictional female job applicants. Two White and two Black applicants submitted their resumes to entry-level retail jobs. Even the White applicant with a criminal record received more call-backs than the Black applicant with no criminal record (Douthwright 2017; cf. Pager 2003). Of the 64 applications submitted by the White applicant with no criminal record, 20 call-backs were received, whereas the White applicant with a criminal record received twelve. By comparison, the Black applicant with no criminal record received only seven call-backs and the Black applicant with a criminal record received just one (Douthwright 2017).

Employment discrimination also affects the income of Black and other racialized Canadians. Data from the 2016 census shows that the income gap for "visible minorities"[2] increased between 2006 and 2016, with members of "visible minority" groups earning on average 26 percent less than non-"visible minorities" (Monsebraaten 2017). Data from the 2006 census highlights the earning gap between Canadian-born "visible minorities" and non-"visible minorities" working similar jobs in Canada's public and private sectors (Hou and Coulombe 2010). While in the public sector, income was similar for members of "visible minority" groups and Whites, that was not the case in the private sector. "Visible minority" men and Black women in particular earned significantly less than Whites in the same industry who were matched in terms of educational attainment and years of professional experience. The income gaps are attributable to inequality of opportunity; the public sector is subject to employment equity regulations, while the private sector faces less pressure in this regard.

Higher unemployment and lower income increase the poverty

2. The Canadian *Employment Equity Act* defines "visible minorities" as "persons, other than Aboriginal persons, who are non-Caucasian in race or non-white in colour." Under this definition, regulations specify that the following groups are included in the visible minority population: Chinese, South Asians, Blacks, Arabs, West Asians, Filipinos, Southeast Asians, Latin Americans, Japanese, Koreans and other visible minority groups, such as Pacific Islanders (Chui, Tran and Maheux, 2008). The visible minority category can be seen as problematic because it lumps diverse racial, ethnic and geographically defined groups into one category, thus masking immense social, cultural and economic differences among them.

rate among Black Canadians. Whereas 6 percent of White Canadian women live below the poverty line, the figure is 25 percent for Black women in Canada. As a result, 33 percent of Black children of Caribbean heritage and 47 percent of those from continental Africa live in poverty (UNHR 2016). The rate for White children is 18 percent. In Toronto, Black Canadians accounted for 19 percent of people living in poverty, more than twice the proportion of the population (National Council of Welfare n.d).

In addition to their individual experiences with poverty, Black Canadians are overrepresented in Toronto neighbourhoods most afflicted by poverty and other forms of disadvantage; household income in neighbourhoods in which Black people are most likely to live increased by just 20 percent from 1980 to 2010. Compounding the effects of lower household incomes, these neighbourhoods are underserved by public transit and have a relatively low concentration of essential services. As a result, Black people in Toronto have poorer access to recreational and community centres, libraries, good schools, community health hubs and hospitals (Hulchanski 2010). These are the very services that serve to create strong communities and protect young people from the allures of crime, gang membership and violence (McMurtry and Curling 2008: 31). In the absence of important social services and in the face of increased poverty, crime and victimization remain high. For example, rates of shooting and homicide are much higher in these neighbourhoods than the city average, and the victims of homicide tend to be younger than for Toronto as a whole (Hulchanski 2010: 23). As noted earlier, young Black men are most adversely affected by this violence—and the ensuing tough enforcement style of policing aimed at targeting its perpetrators (Owusu-Bempah 2014).

Black Canadians and the criminal justice system: Experience and perception

The historical record shows that Black Canadians have had a long and troubled history with the criminal justice system dating back to the 17th century (Mosher 1998; Walker 2010). The historical and contemporary treatment of Black people in the justice system originated in colonialism and slavery, which systematically dehumanized Black Canadians and depicted them as animalistic, aggressive, violent and dangerous (Fishman 2006; Owusu-Bempah 2017). Following the abolition of slavery in 1834, the association of Blackness with criminality and violence was used to control Blacks and justify restrictive immigration practices (Maynard 2017).

Unfortunately, such perceptions have not completely subsided. A tendency in Canada to racialize crime—that is, to develop associations between criminality and racial or ethnic origin—remains (Roberts 2001: 103). A considerable proportion of the Canadian public continues to believe that racialized Canadians are involved in a greater proportion of criminal offences than official statistics show (Rankin and Powell 2008). For example, a 1995 Ontario survey found that nearly one-half of respondents believed that there was an inherent relationship between race and criminality. Of the respondents with this view, two-thirds selected "West Indians" or "Blacks" as being most responsible for crime (Henry et al. 1996: 472).

The continued criminalization of Black people is sustained in part by the manner in which they are depicted in popular media (Welch 2007). A content analysis of stories appearing in Toronto newspapers over a two-month period in 1998 found that almost half the stories featuring Black people dealt with issues relating to crime and violence, compared to only 14 percent of stories featuring Whites (Wortley 2002). Major racial differences in the narratives seeking to explain criminal behaviour were found. While crime involving White people was almost always explained as the product of individual pathology, Black criminality was typically characterized as a group phenomenon (cf. Henry and Tator 2000; Mosher 1998).

In contrast to research on popular perceptions of Black criminality, public perceptions of criminal justice identify bias and discrimination in the system. This is just what the Commission on Systemic Racism in the Ontario Criminal Justice System (1995) found. Its research showed that a considerable proportion of judges and lawyers felt that Black Canadians were treated differently in court than were White Canadians (Commission on Systemic Racism 1995). Members of the public were also asked about bias in both policing and the criminal court system. The Commission's survey found that over half of Black, White and Chinese respondents Toronto believed that the police treated Black people differently than White people. Similarly, more than one-half of Black respondents and one-third of White and Chinese respondents felt that Black people are treated differently in the courts.

This study was replicated in 2007. Despite myriad "race relations" initiatives that had been implemented over the preceding decade, the more recent study found that perceptions of bias *increased* among Black and White respondents. Thus, in 1994, 76 percent of Black respondents felt that the police treated Black people worse or much worse than Whites. By 2007 this figure rose to 81 percent. Similarly, in 1994, 48 percent of Black respondents believed that a Black person would get a longer sentence than a White person charged with the same crime. In 2007, this figure rose to 58 percent (Wortley and Owusu-Bempah 2009: 465).

Citizens' perceptions of criminal injustice constitute an important social issue. The police and court system rely on citizens to act as witnesses and co-operate as victims, but mounting evidence suggests that negative views of the criminal justice system contribute to criminal offending (Tyler 1988; 2003; Tyler and Fagan 2008). People who view the system as unjust are less likely to believe they should abide by the system's rules (Tyler 2003). This is particularly salient in the current context. As Black people are more likely than members of other racial groups to perceive the justice system as discriminatory, they are also more likely to participate in what might be thought of as system-generated offending behaviour.

Likewise, evidence suggests that Black youth engage in violence as a means of "self-help" resulting from the belief that the police cannot or will not provide adequate protection. One study found that gun carrying among Black youth results from fear of victimization and a feeling that the police cannot act as capable guardians (Wilkinson, Beaty and Lurry 2009: 29-31). The perception that they must take the law into their own hands not only adds to the cycle of violence in disadvantaged neighbourhoods but also increases the risk of criminalization for Black youth when they encounter the police.

We next examine evidence of Black overrepresentation in three aspects of the delivery of the criminal justice in Ontario. These practices have troubling consequences for the incarceration rate of young Black Canadian men.

Police stop-and-search practices

Survey research conducted over the past two decades consistently demonstrates that Black Canadians are more likely than members of other racial groups to be stopped, searched and questioned by the police. For instance, a 1994 survey of Torontonians found that almost one-third of Black male respondents had been stopped and questioned by the police on two or more occasions in the previous two years, compared with only 12 percent of White and 7 percent of Asian males (Wortley and Tanner 2003: 371). These racial differences could not be explained by racial differences in social class, education or other important socio-demographic variables. In fact, age and class, which shield White males from police contact, fail to provide Blacks with the same protection. Thus, White people with higher levels of income and education are less likely to be stopped by the police than are White people with lower income and level of education. In contrast, Black people with higher levels of income and education are more likely to be stopped than Black people with lower income and level of education (Wortley and Tanner 2003: 371).

Another Toronto survey involving youth paints a similar picture. The researchers asked Toronto high school students about their recent experiences with the police. They found that over 50 percent of the Black students reported being been stopped and questioned by the police on two or more occasions in the previous two years, compared to only 23 percent of White, 11 percent of Asian, and 8 percent of South Asian students. Similarly, over 40 percent of Black students said that they had been searched by the police in the previous two years, compared to only 17 percent of their White and 11 percent of their Asian counterparts. Racial differences in being stopped and searched by the police could not be explained by racial differences in criminal activity, gang membership, drug and alcohol use or public leisure activities (Wortley and Tanner 2005). Yet another survey found that Black adult Toronto residents were three times more likely than their White counterparts to be stopped and searched by police in the previous two years and that this racial disparity could not be explained by racial differences in criminality, drug and alcohol use, driving habits, use of public spaces, poverty or residence in a high-crime community (Wortley and Owusu-Bempah 2011).

A source of police information that has gained much public attention in recent years comprises "contact card" or "street check" data collected by police officers in the course of their duties. These data are not collected by police in every civilian encounter, just those for which an officer wants to record information for intelligence purposes. In addition to details about police stops, contact card and streets checks also typically garner demographic information about the civilian, including age, race and gender. "Carding" offers insight into police surveillance practices that typically target individuals and neighbourhoods subject to a high level of police scrutiny (Owusu-Bempah and Wortley 2014).

Data from across Ontario demonstrate that Black people are overrepresented in carding (Bennett 2015; Grewal 2015; O'Brien 2016; Rankin 2010b; Sharkey 2016; Yogaretham 2015). The *Toronto Star's* analysis of over 1.7 million contact cards filled out by Toronto police between 2003 and 2008 found that Black people comprised almost 25 percent of the carded population. Black overrepresentation in carding is evident throughout the city, regardless of neighbourhood crime rate and racial composition (Rankin 2010a; 2010b).

Targeting of Black Canadians by the police has two main consequences for Black communities. First, because Black people are exposed to high levels of police surveillance, they are much more likely to be caught breaking the law than are White people who engage in the same behaviours. A Toronto high school survey found that 65 percent of Black drug dealers (youth who reported selling drugs on ten or more occasions in the previous twelve months) said they had been arrested in their lifetime, compared to 35 percent of White drug dealers (Wortley and Tanner 2005: 586). Between 2003 and 2013, Black people accounted for 26 percent of people arrested for cannabis possession by the Toronto Police Service, with cannabis arrests increasing in tandem with carding (Rankin and Contenta 2017). Evidence suggests that rates of cannabis use are similar across racial groups (Hamilton et al. 2018), so race-based targeting may help explain why Black people are overrepresented in arrests for cannabis possession.

A second important consequence of differential police stop-and-search practices is that they contribute to perceptions of criminal and social injustice. Research shows that Black people who are frequently stopped and questioned by police perceive much higher levels of bias and discrimination in the Canadian criminal justice system than do Black people who are not frequently stopped (Wortley and Owusu-Bempah 2011). The practice may signal to Black people that, irrespective of individual behaviour, being Black means being considered one of the usual suspects.

Pre-trial decision making

As gatekeepers of the criminal justice system, the police influence who is officially processed by that system. Here, racial disparities at the front end in stop-and-search and other areas of decision making can have serious consequences. Unfortunately, little race-based data on pre-trial decision making is available in the Canadian context. An analysis of Toronto Police data shows that Black people are not only overrepresented in drug possession charges but are also less likely to be released by the police at the scene than White people. The data indicate that the proportion of White people arrested on one count of simple drug possession was about the same as the proportion of White people in the population, while the proportion of Black people arrested on the same charge was around three times their representation in the population. More than three-quarters of White people accused of drug possession were released at the scene. The same was true for only six of ten Blacks (Rankin et al. 2002a; 2002b).

Pre-trial detention rates also vary between the two groups; 15 percent of Black accused were held until trial compared to 7 percent of Whites. These findings held even after controlling for other relevant factors (Rankin et al. 2002a; 2002b). Further evidence of racial disparity in pre-trial decision-making comes from a study that tracked over 1,800 criminal cases from two Toronto bail courts during a six-month period in 1994 (Kellough and Wortley 2002). The findings indicate that 36 percent of Black accused were detained before trial compared to 23 percent of accused from other racial backgrounds. Again, race remained a significant factor even after controlling for relevant factors such as flight risk and danger to the public.

Data from the Ontario Ministry of Community Safety and Correctional Services shows that Black accused are detained longer before trial than White accused (Mehler Paperny 2017). It is important to note that the denial of bail has serious consequences for the accused. First, it might be used as a way to coerce guilty pleas from individuals who are reluctant to be held in detention centres for extended periods. Second, individuals who have been denied bail receive longer custodial sentences than individuals who are found guilty but were not held in remand before their trial (Sacks and Ackerman 2014: 69).

Incarceration

Despite a declining inmate population overall, the number of Black inmates in Canadian federal correctional institutions increased 75 percent from 2002 to 2012. Whereas Black Canadians represent just 2.9 percent of the Canadian population, they accounted for 9.3 percent of the federal prison population (Office of the Correctional Investigator 2013). Of concern is both the increasing representation of Black Canadians in federal custody and their treatment in these institutions (Office of the Correctional Investigator 2013). Based on consultations with Black inmates and a review of correctional data, the Office of the Correctional Investigator (OCI) produced a detailed report that documents the inequalities faced by Black inmates (Office of the Correctional Investigator 2013; the Office of the Correctional Investigator acts as the ombudsperson for federal prisoners).

The OCI found that Black inmates consistently reported that institutional rules are applied differently to them when compared with Whites and inmates from other racial groups. Between 2007-08 and 2011-12, the number of Black inmates facing disciplinary charges increased 59 percent, while the overall number of disciplinary charges laid over the same period dropped by 7 percent. Black inmates were consistently overrepresented in charges requiring judgement on the part of correctional officers, while they were consistently underrepresented in less discretionary charge categories (such as possession of stolen property, theft and damage of property) (Office of the Correctional Investigator 2013: 22).

Furthermore, between 2009 and 2013, despite being classified as having lower risk/needs scores, Black inmates were more likely than their White counterparts to be placed in maximum security and are less likely to have their custody score lowered so they can be transferred to medium or minimum security prisons (Office of the Correctional Investigator 2013: 21). This pattern suggests that at some point between risk classification and prison placement, Black inmates are classified as higher risk and deserving maximum security, and at no point does it appear that this assessment was reversed. The OCI has also found that Black inmates are overrepresented in admissions to segregation and disproportionately involved in use-of-force incidents. Whereas Black inmates accounted for 9.3 percent of the total inmate population in 2011-12 they accounted for 11.7 percent of inmates placed in involuntary segregation (Office of the Correctional Investigator 2013: 23). In 2012-13 Black inmates were involved in 13 percent of use-of-force incidents.

The bulk of evidence from the OCI report suggests that Black inmates are often not treated with dignity and respect by CSC staff. Evidence also suggests that mistreatment is tied to aspects of the inmates' culture (language, dress and so on) and where Black inmates lived prior to incarceration. Black inmates provided examples of overhearing CSC staff mocking the way they spoke or trying to speak with a Jamaican accent to their colleagues. One inmate reported a correctional officer asking him "What is wrong with your tongue, don't talk to me like a hoodlum" (Office of the Correctional Investigator 2013: 19).

Black inmates also reported numerous examples of stereotyping. Judgments about character and lifestyle were also common. Most Black men described being labeled a "gang member," "troublemaker," "drug dealer" and/or "womanizer" (Office of the Correctional Investigator 2013: 17). Among Black inmates, "the gang member/

affiliation stereotype" was of "particular concern" (Office of the Correctional Investigator 2013: 19). During focus groups, Black inmates reported that the gang label hindered their ability to obtain access to CORCAN jobs (CORCAN is an agency that "offers employment training and employability skills to offenders in federal correctional institutions, to support rehabilitation and help lower rates of re-offending;" Office of the Correctional Investigator 2016). This predicament leaves them working jobs that provided little valuable experience that would aid their re-entry into society. Thus, while the unemployment rate inside federal correctional facilities was 1.5 percent in 2012–13, the unemployment rate for Black inmates was 7 percent (Office of the Correctional Investigator 2013: 20).

Black overrepresentation in corrections is also apparent at the provincial level. In 2010, Black adults accounted for 18 percent of admissions to provincial custody (Owusu-Bempah and Wortley 2014). Similarly, in 2011–12, Black youth accounted for 24 percent of admissions to custody in Ontario (Rankin and Winsa 2013). The incarceration rate for young men has steadily declined since the introduction of the Youth Criminal Justice Act in 2003, but Black male youth have not benefitted from this decline. In fact, evidence from the federal and provincial correctional systems indicates that incarceration is becoming increasingly concentrated among certain racialized groups, and in specific geographical areas, and that Black Canadians have been disproportionately affected by these trends (Office of the Correctional Investigator 2013; Owusu-Bempah and Wortley 2014).

The impact of incarceration

For individuals, incarceration significantly reduces later employment rates and income levels (Freeman 1992). Incarceration also has a significant negative influence on social networks, social relationships and long-term life chances, thus impacting one's ability to contribute to family and community (Clear 2008; Robert, 2004). The families of those incarcerated also suffer financial and emotional costs related to separation, the loss of income and the need to support an imprisoned family member (Braman 2002; Wildeman et al. 2012).

Evidence suggests that arrests disrupt marital relationships, separate children from parents and can result in the permanent dissolution of these relationships (Christian 2004). Research also shows that children with parents in prison suffer serious psychological consequences, including depression, anxiety, feelings of rejection, shame, anger and guilt (Browning et al. 2001). These children are also more likely to experience school failure, under-employment and illegal drug use (Clear 2008).

The impact of concentrated incarceration clearly extends from the family unit into the community. Because going to prison permanently influences employment and earning potential, it also damages the labour prospects of young people in a community by decreasing the pool of individuals who can act as mentors and social contacts (Sabol and Lynch 2004). A reduction in the number of people engaged in the labour market affects the local economy because individuals have less money to spend at local establishments (Sullivan 1989; Venkatesh 1997). Concentrated incarceration also distorts norms, leads to the breakdown of informal social control and therefore undermines the building blocks of social order that are essential for community safety (Clear 2002).

In sum, concentrated incarceration exacerbates social problems, fostering a cycle of inequities in communities and across generations. The fact that incarceration is becoming increasingly concentrated among Black Canadians reproduces and worsens conditions that contribute to incarceration in the first place.

Remedies

In a country as diverse and inclusive as ours, much can be done to reduce the burden of incarceration faced by African Canadians. The recent introduction of Impact of Race and Culture Assessments (IRCAs) into the sentencing process presents one possibility for reform. IRCAs are intended to provide the court with comprehensive information about how an individual's experiences with racism and socio-economic disadvantage have influenced their offending behaviour and subsequent contact with the criminal justice system. IRCAs have been successfully used in court cases involving African Canadian offenders in Nova Scotia and Ontario. In these cases, defence counsel successfully argued for sentences that fell toward the bottom or below the accepted sentencing range for the crime in question. These cases signal an acceptance from the sentencing judges that the actions of the offenders were influenced, at least in part, by racism and marginalization experienced in Canadian society.

IRCAs hold promise for reforming sentencing practices. However, they are unlikely to dramatically reduce overrepresentation of African Canadians in the criminal justice system because they are employed at the back end, following conviction (and by extension, one's criminalization). To substantially reduce overincarceration, we must work to increase the participation of African Canadians in the social, political and economic life of the country. Their overrepresentation in Canadian prisons is a manifestation of their marginalization, second only to that of the nation's Indigenous population, another group that is heavily over-criminalized. Until Canada reckons with its history and acknowledges how that history influences the contemporary experience of Black Canadians, over-incarceration will continue to be a feature of the Black experience in this country.

References

Anderson, Elijah. 1999. *Code of the Street: Decency, Violence and the Moral Life of the Inner City*. New York: W.W. Norton.

Bennett, K. 2015. Hamilton police disproportionately stop and question black people. *CBC News*. http://www.cbc.ca/news/canada/hamilton/news/hamilton-police-disproportionately-stop-and-question-Black-people-1.3165182.

Braman, D. 2002. *Families and Incarceration*. PhD dissertation, Yale University.

Browning, S. L., Miller, R. R. and Spruance, L. M. 2001. Criminal incarceration dividing the ties that bind: Black men and their families. *Journal of African American Men* 6(1): 87–102.

Children's Aid Society of Toronto. 2015. *Children's Aid Society of Toronto: Black African Caribbean Canadian Committee Community Consultations: Spring and Fall 2015: Purpose, Findings and Recommendations*. http://www.torontocas.ca/sites/torontocas/files/CAST_CommConsultRecommendationsMay2016.pdf.

Chui, T., Tran, K., and Maheux, H. 2008. *Canada's Ethnocultural Mosaic: The 2006 Census*. Catalogue no. 97-562-X. Ottawa: Statistics Canada.

Christian, J. R. 2004. *Exploring the Effects of Incarceration on Communities*. PhD dissertation, School of Criminal Justice, University at Albany.

CivicAction. 2014. Creating New Paths to Employment for Youth. http://www.civicaction.ca/creatingnewemployment/.

Clear, T. R. 2002. The problem with 'addition by subtraction': the prison-crime relationship in low-income communities. Pp. 181–94 in M. Mauer and M. Chesney-Lind, eds. *Invisible Punishment: The Collateral Consequences of Mass Imprisonment*. New York: New Press.

Cole, D. 2020. *The Skin We're in: A Year of Black Resistance and Power*. Toronto: Penguin Random House Canada.

Commission on Systemic Racism in the Ontario Criminal Justice System. 1995. *Report of the Commission on Systemic Racism in the Ontario Criminal Justice System*. Toronto: Queen's Printer for Ontario.

Connell, R. W. 2005. Growing up masculine: rethinking the significance of adolescence in the making of masculinities. *Irish Journal of Sociology* (14(2): 11–28.

Connell, R. W. and Messerschmidt, J. W. 2005. Hegemonic masculinity: rethinking the concept. *Gender and Society* 19(6): 829–59.

Connell, R.W. 2005. *Masculinities*, 2nd ed. Berkeley: University of California Press.

Correctional Service of Canada. 2016. *CORCAN – Employment and Employability*. Available: http://www.csc-scc.gc.ca/publications/005007-3016-eng.shtml.

Cruickshank, A. 2017. Black job seekers have harder time finding retail and service work than their white counterparts, study suggests. *Toronto Star*, 26 December. https://www.thestar.com/news/gta/2017/12/26/black-job-seekers-have-harder-time-finding-retail-and-service-work-than-their-white-counterparts-study-suggests.html.

Dei, G. J. S. and Kempf, A. 2013. *New Perspectives on African-centred Education in Canada.* Toronto: Canadian Scholars' Press.

Douthwright, J. 2017. *Employer Discrimination Against Applicants with Criminal Records: An Audit Study.* MA Thesis, Centre for Criminology and Sociolegal Studies, University of Toronto.

Eberhardt, J. L., Goff, P. A., Purdie, V. J. and Davies, P. G. 2004. Seeing Black: race, crime, and visual processing. *Journal of Personality and Social Psychology* 87(6): 876–93.

Environics Institute. 2019. *Race Relations in Canada 2019.* https://www.environicsinstitute.org/docs/default-source/project-documents/race-relations-2019-survey/race-relations-in-canada-2019-survey---final-report-english.pdf?sfvrsn=ef8d61e3_2.

Fallon, B., Van Wert, M., Trocmé, N., MacLaurin, B., Sinha, V., Lefebvre, R., Allan, K., Black, T., Less, B., Rha, W., Smith, C., Goel, S. 2015. *Ontario Incidence Study of Reported Child Abuse and Neglect 2013.* Canadian Child Welfare Research Portal. https://cwrp.ca/publications/ontario-incidence-study-reported-child-abuse-and-neglect-2013-ois-2013.

Fishman, L.T. 2006 The Black bogeyman and White self-righteousness. Pp. 197-211 in C.R. Mann, M.S. Zatz and N. Rodriguez eds. *Images of Color, Images of Crime.* New York: Oxford University Press.

Gartner, R. and Thompson, S. 2004. Trends in Homicide in Toronto. Pp. 24–39 in *From Enforcement to Prevention to Civic Engagement: Research on Community Safety,* Bruce Kidd and Jim Phillips, ed. Toronto: Centre of Criminology, University of Toronto.

Goff, P. A., Leone, D., Lewis, B. A. and Kahn, K. B. 2012. Racism leads to pushups: how racial discrimination threatens subordinate men's masculinity. *Journal of Experimental Social Psychology* 48(5): 1111–16.

Goff, P. A., Steele, C. M. and Davies, P. G. 2008. The space between us: stereotype threat and distance in interracial contexts. *Journal of Personality and Social Psychology,* 94(1): 91–107.

Grewal, S. 2015. Blacks three times more likely to be carded by Peel police than whites. *Toronto Star,* 24 September. https://www.thestar.com/news/gta/2015/09/24/blacks-three-times-more-likely-to-be-carded-by-peel-police-than-whites.html.

Groes-Green, C. 2009. Hegemonic and subordinated masculinities: class, violence and sexual performance among young Mozambican men. *Nordic Journal of African Studies* 18(4): 286–304.

Groot, W. and van den Brink, H. M. 2010. The effects of education on crime. *Applied Economics* 42(3): 279–89.

Hamilton, H. A., Owusu-Bempah, A., Boak, A. and Mann, R. E. 2018. Ethnoracial differences in cannabis use among native-born and foreign-born high school students in Ontario. *Journal of Ethnicity in Substance Abuse* 17(2): 123–34.

Hawkins, J. D., Herrenkohl, T. I., Farrington, D. P., Brewer, D., Catalano, R. F., Harachi, T. W. and Cothern, L. 2000. *Predictors of Youth Violence.*

OJJDP Juvenile Justice Bulletin. Washington, DC: US Department of Justice.

Henry, F. and Ginzberg, E. 1985. *Who Gets the Work? A Test of Racial Discrimination in Employment.* Toronto: Urban Alliance on Race Relations and the Social Planning Council of Metropolitan Toronto.

Henry, F. and Tator, C. 2005. *The Colour of Democracy: Racism in Canadian Society,* 3rd ed. Toronto: Nelson.

Henry, F., Hastings, P. and Freer, B. 1996. Perceptions of race and crime in Ontario: empirical evidence from Toronto and the Durham Region. *Canadian Journal of Criminology* 38(4): 469–76.

Hope, D.P. 2010. *Man Vibes: Masculinities in the Jamaican Dancehall.* Kingston JA: Ian Randle Publishers.

Hou, F. and Coulombe, S. 2010. Earnings gaps for Canadian-born visible minorities in the public and private sectors. *Canadian Public Policy* 36(1): 29–43.

Hulchanski, J. D. 2010. *The Three Cities within Toronto.* Toronto: Cities Centre.

James, C. E. 1998. 'Up to no good': Black on the streets and encountering police. Pp. 157–76 in V. Satzewich ed. *Racism and Social Inequality in Canada: Concepts, Controversies and Strategies of Resistance.* Toronto: Thompson.

James, C.E. 2009. Masculinity, racialization and schooling: the making of marginalized men. Pp. 102–23 in W. Martino, W. Kehler and M. Weaver-Hightower, eds. *The Problem with Boys' Education: Beyond the Backlash.* New York: Routledge.

James, C.E. 2012. Students at risk: stereotyping and the schooling of Black boys. *Urban Education* 47(2): 464–94.

James, C.E. 2018. "Singled out": being a Black youth in the suburbs. Pp. 133–51 in L. Foster, L. Jacobs and B. Siu, eds. *Racial Profiling and Human Rights in Canada: The New Legal Landscape.* Toronto: Irwin Law.

James, C. E. and Turner, T. 2017. *Towards Race Equity in Education: The Schooling of Black Students in the Greater Toronto Area.* Toronto: York University.

Jonson-Reid, M. and Barth, R. P. 2000. From placement to prison: the path to adolescent incarceration from child welfare supervised foster or group care. *Children and Youth Services Review* 22(7): 493–516.

Kellough, G. and Wortley, S. 2002. Remand for plea. Bail decisions and plea bargaining as commensurate decisions. *British Journal of Criminology* 42(1): 186–210.

Khenti, A. 2013. Homicide among young Black men in Toronto: An unrecognized public health crisis. *Canadian Journal of Public Health* 104(1): 12–14.

Kimmel, M. 2008. *Guyland: The Perilous World where Boys Become Men* New York: HarperCollins.

King, B., Fallon, B., Boyd, R., Black, T., Antwi-Boasiako, K. and O'Connor, C. 2017. Factors associated with racial differences in child welfare investigative decision-making in Ontario, Canada. *Child Abuse and Neglect* 73: 89–105.

Kochel, T. R., Wilson, D. B. and Mastrofski, S. D. 2011. Effect of suspect race on officers' arrest decisions. *Criminology* 49(2): 473–512.

Krohn, M. D. 1976. Inequality, unemployment and crime: a cross-national analysis. *The Sociological Quarterly* 17(3): 303–13.

Leach, M. 1994. The politics of masculinity: an overview of contemporary theory. *Social Alternatives* 12(4): 36–7.

Lewis, S. 1992. *Stephen Lewis Report on Race Relations in Ontario.* Toronto: Government of Ontario.

Lochner, L. and Moretti, E. 2004. The effect of education on crime: evidence from prison inmates, arrests, and self-Reports. *American Economic Review* 94(1): 155–89.

Lynch, J. P. and Sabol, W. J. 2004. Assessing the effects of mass incarceration on informal social control in communities. *Criminology and Public Policy* 3(2): 267–94.

Majors, R. and Billson, J. M. 1992. *Cool Pose.* New York: Lexington.

Maynard, R. 2017. *Policing Black Lives.* Halifax: Fernwood .

McMurtry, R. and Curling, A. 2008. *The Review of the Roots of Youth Violence,* vol. 1. Toronto: Service Ontario Publications.

Mehler Paperny, A. 2017. Exclusive: New data shows race disparities in Canada's bail system. *Reuters,* 19 October. https://ca.reuters.com/article/domesticNews/idCAKBN1CO2RD-OCADN.

Messerschmidt, J. W. 2000. *Nine Lives: Adolescent Masculinities, the Body, and Violence.* Boulder CO: Westview Press.

Monsebraaten, L. 2017. Income gap persists for recent immigrants, visible minorities and Indigenous Canadians. *Toronto Star,* 25 October. https://www.thestar.com/news/gta/2017/10/25/income-gap-persists-for-recent-immigrants-visible-minorities-and-indigenous-canadians.html.

Morgan, A. 2016. *The Blackening Margins of Multiculturalism: The African Canadian Experience of Exclusion from the Economic, Social and Cultural Promise and Prosperity of Canada.* Toronto: The African Canadian Legal Clinic.

Mosher, C. 1998. *Discrimination and Denial: Systemic Racism in Ontario's Legal and Criminal Justice Systems, 1892–1961.* Toronto: University of Toronto Press.

National Council of Welfare. n.d. *A Snapshot of Racialized Poverty in Canada.* https://www.canada.ca/content/dam/esdc-edsc/migration/documents/eng/communities/reports/poverty_profile/snapshot.pdf.

O'Brien, J. 2016. London's rate of conducting street checks is three times that of Ottawa and Hamilton. *London Free Press,* 24 June. http://www.lfpress.com/2015/06/24/londons-rate-of-conducting-street-checks-is-three-times-that-of-ottawa-and-hamilton.

Office of the Correctional Investigator. 2013. *A Case Study of Diversity in Corrections: The Black Inmate Experience in Federal Penitentiaries.*

http://www.oci-bec.gc.ca/cnt/rpt/pdf/oth-aut/oth-aut20131126-eng.
pdf.

Office of the Correctional Investigator. 2016. *Annual Report of the Office of the Correctional Investigator 2015–2016.* https://www.oci-bec.gc.ca/cnt/rpt/pdf/annrpt/annrpt20152016-eng.pdf.

Ontario Association of Children's Aid Societies. 2016. *One Vision One Voice: Changing the Ontario Child Welfare System to Better Serve African Canadians.* Toronto: Ontario Association of Children's Aid Societies.

Ontario Human Rights Commission. 2018. *Interrupted Childhoods: Over-representation of Indigenous and Black Children in Ontario Child Welfare.* http://www.ohrc.on.ca/en/interrupted-childhoods.

Owusu-Bempah, A. 2014. *Black Males' Perceptions of and Experiences with the Police in Toronto.* PhD dissertation, University of Toronto.

Owusu-Bempah, A. 2017. Race and policing in historical context: dehumanization and the policing of Black people in the 21st century. *Theoretical Criminology* 21(1): 23–34.

Owusu-Bempah, A and S. Wortley. 2014. Race, crime, and criminal justice in Canada. Pp. 281–320 in S. Bucerius and M. Tonry, eds. *The Oxford Handbook on Race, Ethnicity, Crime, and Immigration.* New York: Oxford University Press.

Owusu-Bempah, K. 2007. *Children and Separation: Socio-Genealogical Connectedness Perspective.* London: Routledge.

Owusu-Bempah, K. 2010. *The Wellbeing of Children in Care: A New Approach for Improving Developmental Outcomes.* London: Routledge.

Owusu-Bempah, J. and Howitt, D. 1997. Socio-genealogical connectedness, attachment theory, and childcare practice. *Child and Family Social Work* 2(4): 199–207.

Pager, D. 2003. The mark of a criminal record. *American Journal of Sociology* 108(5): 937–75.

Patriquin, M. 2007. Canada: a nation of bigots? *Maclean's,* 22 October, *120*(41): 17–18, 20–22.

Powell, B. 2008. Police hampered by code of silence. *Toronto Star,* 8 January. http://www.thestar.com/news/gta/2008/01/02/police_hampered_by_code_of_silence.html.

Puxley, C. 2007. Ontario to scrap zero-tolerance at schools. *Toronto Star,* 10 April. http://www.thestar.com/news/2007/04/10/ontario_to_scrap_zerotolerance_at_schools.html

Rankin, J. 2010a. When good people are swept up with the bad. *Toronto Star,* 6 February: A1.

Rankin, J. 2010b, February 6. CARDED: Probing a racial disparity. *Toronto Star,* 6 February: IN1.

Rankin, J., Contenta, S. and Bailey, A. 2017. Toronto marijuana arrests reveal 'startling' racial divide. *Toronto Star,* 6 July. https://www.thestar.com/news/insight/2017/07/06/toronto-marijuana-arrests-reveal-startling-racial-divide.html.

Rankin, J. and Winsa, P. 2013. Unequal justice: Aboriginal and black inmates disproportionately fill Ontario jails. *Toronto Star*, 1 March. http://www.thestar.com/news/insight/2013/03/01/unequal_justice_aboriginal_and_black_inmates_disproportionately_fill_ontario_jails.html.

Rankin, J., Quinn, J., Shephard, M., Simmie, S. and Duncanson, J. 2002a. Singled out: an investigation into race and crime. *Toronto Star*, 19 October: A1. https://www.thestar.com/news/gta/knowntopolice/2002/10/19/singled-out.html.

Rankin, J., Quinn, J., Shephard, M., Simmie, S. and Duncanson, J. 2002b. Singled out. *Toronto Star*, 20 October: A1. https://www.thestar.com/news/gta/knowntopolice/2002/10/19/singled-out.html.

Roberts, D. 2002. *Shattered Bonds: The Color of Child Welfare*. New York: Basic Civitas Books.

Roberts, J.V. 2001. *Race, Crime and the Collection of Criminal Justice Statistics*. Pp. 102-11 in Chan, W. and Mirchandi, K. eds. *Crimes of Colour. Racialization and the Criminal Justice System*. Peterborough: Broadview Press.

Sacks, M. and Ackerman, A. R. 2014. Bail and sentencing: does pretrial detention lead to harsher punishment? *Criminal Justice Policy Review* 25(1): 59–77.

Sharkey, J. 2016. Carding: who gets stopped for street checks in Waterloo Region. *CBC News*, 9 April. http://www.cbc.ca/news/canada/kitchener-waterloo/carding-street-checks-waterloo-region-1.3527657.

Statistics Canada. 2017a. Ethnic and cultural origins of Canadians: Portrait of a rich heritage. https://www12.statcan.gc.ca/census-recensement/2016/as-sa/98-200-x/2016016/98-200-x2016016-eng.cfm.

Statistics Canada. 2017b. Stats Can (2017) Linguistic diversity and multilingualism in Canadian homes. https://www12.statcan.gc.ca/census-recensement/2016/as-sa/98-200-x/2016010/98-200-x2016010-eng.pdf.

Statistics Canada. 2020. Estimates of the components of international migration, quarterly. https://www150.statcan.gc.ca/t1/tbl1/en/tv.action?pid=1710004001.

Tanner, J. and Wortley, S. 2002. *The Toronto Youth Crime and Victimization Survey: Overview Report*. Toronto: Centre of Criminology, University of Toronto.

Tecle, S. and James, C. E., 2014. Refugee students in Canadian schools: educational issues and challenges. Pp. 147–61 in C.A. Brewer and M. McCabe, eds. *Immigrant and Refugee Students in Canada*. Edmonton, AB: Brush Education Inc.

Tyler, T. R. 1988. What is procedural justice? criteria used by citizens to assess the fairness of legal procedures. *Law and Society Review* 22(1): 103–36.

Tyler, T. R. 2003. Procedural justice, legitimacy, and the effective rule of law. *Crime and Justice* 30: 283–357.

Tyler, T. R. and Fagan, J. 2008. Legitimacy and cooperation: why do people help the police fight crime in their communities? *Ohio State Journal of*

Criminal Law 6: 231–75.

United Nations Human Rights Office of the High Commissioner 2016. Statement to the media by the United Nations' Working Group of Experts on People of African Descent, on the conclusion of its official visit to Canada, 17–21 October 2016. http://www.ohchr.org/EN/NewsEvents/Pages/DisplayNews.aspx?NewsID=20732.

Vecchio, K. 1998. Dismantling white male privilege within family therapy. Pp. 159–75 in M. McGoldrick ed. *Revisioning Family Therapy*. New York: New York University Press.

Venkatesh, S. 1997. The social organization of street gang activity in an urban ghetto. *American Journal of Sociology* 103(1): 82–111.

Walker, B. 2010. *Race on Trial: Black Defendants in Ontario's Criminal Courts, 1858–1958*. Toronto: University of Toronto Press.

Ward, J. V. 1996. Raising resisters: the role of truth telling in the psychological development of African American girls. Pp. 85–9 in B.J. Leadbeater and N. Way, eds. *Urban Girls Resisting Stereotypes, Creating Identities*. New York: New York University Press.

Welch, K. 2007. Black criminal stereotypes and racial profiling. *Journal of Contemporary Criminal Justice* 23(3): 276–88.

Wildeman, C., Schnittker, J. and Turney, K. 2012. Despair by association? the mental health of mothers with children by recently incarcerated fathers. *American Sociological Review* 77(2): 216–43.

Wilkinson, D. L., Beaty, C. C. and Lurry, R. M. 2009. Youth violence—crime or self-help? marginalized urban males' perspectives on the limited efficacy of the criminal justice system to stop youth violence. *Annals of the American Academy of Political and Social Science* 623(1): 25–38.

Winks, R. 1997. *The Blacks in Canada*. Montreal: McGill-Queen's University Press.

Wortley, S. 2002. Misrepresentation or reality? misrepresentation, race and crime in the Toronto Print Media. Pp. 55–82 in Brooks, C., and B. Schissel, eds. *Marginality and Condemnation: An Introduction to Criminology*. Halifax: Fernwood.

Wortley, S. 2008. A province at the crossroads: statistics on youth violence in Ontario. Pp. 1–64 in *Review of the Roots of Youth Violence, Vol. Five*, R. McMurtry and A. Curling, eds. Toronto: Queen's Printer for Ontario.

Wortley, S. and Owusu-Bempah, A. 2009. Unequal before the law: Immigrant and racial minority perceptions of the Canadian criminal justice system. *Journal of International Migration and Integration, 104*, 447–473.

Wortley, S. and Owusu-Bempah, A. 2011. The usual suspects: police stop and search practices in Canada. *Policing and Society* 21(4): 395–407.

Wortley, S. and Tanner, J. 2003. Data, denials, and confusion: the racial profiling debate in Toronto. *Canadian Journal of Criminology and Criminal Justice* 45(3): 367-90.

Wortley, S. and Tanner, J. 2005. Inflammatory rhetoric? baseless accusations? a response to Gabor's critique of racial profiling research in Canada. *Canadian Journal of Criminology and Criminal Justice*, 47(3): 581–610.

Yogaretnan. S. 2015. Street checks data about racialized men concerning to civil liberties advocates. *Ottawa Citizen*, 26 July. http://ottawacitizen.com/news/local-news/street-checks-data-about-racialized-men-concerning-to-civil-liberties-advocates.

CHAPTER FOUR

Antisemitism in Canada: Past, Present and Future

Morton Weinfeld[1]

This paper presents data and interpretation concerning antisemitism in Canada. First, two personal notes. In the 1980s, Canadian immigration totals were low, around 80,000 per year. I felt Canada should and could increase that amount, and not be deterred by an influx of non-Europeans. I began to develop that position in op-eds, reports and academic articles. As part of the immigration debate, the issue of racism loomed large. Many policy makers were apprehensive. They worried about existing and growing racism and Balkanization of immigrant communities—Chinese malls, and perhaps the emergence of racist populist parties like the *Front National* in France. I argued that Canadian racism was not that formidable. It would not grow in scope and Canada need not fear more non-European migration. Non-European immigrants were integrating and would continue to integrate well. Canada's immigrant intake increased steadily and is now around 300,000 per year. Was I wrong then about conditions at the time, or about how they would evolve?

Fast forward to September 2019. Attending my Montreal synagogue for the Jewish New Year, I observed dramatically ramped-up security. Two large concrete slabs had been placed near the walkway into the building to prevent cars from getting close. And instead of one young unarmed guard as typical on the Sabbath, there were three experienced (but still unarmed) guards stationed at the entrance. For years, synagogues in Europe have had far greater security. In January 2020 the synagogue posted the following sign near the entrance: "Do not hold the door open for a stranger. This is not being rude; it is being safe." These kinds of steps may be the new Canadian normal.

---

1. I thank Mr. Jonah Levitt for editorial and bibliographic assistance.

Historical background

Antisemitism dates back to the slavery of the Jews in Egypt. Pharaoh regarded them as a suspect minority (Exodus 1: 10). It continues through the Roman conquest, which involved putting an end to Jewish sovereignty by means of murder, exile, enslavement and the destruction of the Second Temple in Jerusalem. Two thousand years of subsequent minority diasporic experience, while by no means uniformly dismal, featured major eruptions of Jew hatred, murder and exile, from the beginning of the First Crusade in 1096 through the Spanish Inquisition in the late 1400s and Eastern European pogroms in the 19th and early 20th centuries. The horror of the Holocaust casts a deep shadow on contemporary Jewish attitudes about antisemitism.

Because of this history, antisemitism, whether real or potential, is a constant feature of modern life for Jews. Hence the grim Jewish quip: "An antisemite is someone who hates Jews more than absolutely necessary." Even before the discovery of micro-aggressions, many Jews in Western diasporas kept their antennae tuned to "high," alert to possible slights and warning signals (Seeley et al. 1956; Sklare and Greenblum 1967).

Thus, vigilance takes precedence over complacency. Most Canadian Jews know that many Jews living in Weimar Germany were highly assimilated, devoted to Germany and German culture. In 1933, the Jewish intermarriage was 28 percent (Lowenstein 2005: 26). None of this prevented the rise of Nazism. Jewish communal discourse is often shaped by post-Holocaust subliminal questions like, "Could it happen here?" and admonitions like "Never again."

The Jewish experience in Canada varies by region, with large differences between Quebec and the rest of Canada. The Jewish experience in Canada also varies by migration status, gender and social class, but these factors will not be explored in great detail here. With steady post-World War II upward mobility, Jews became increasingly "white," meaning they were less frequently victimized than racialized groups were (for another interpretation of increasing Jewish whiteness, see Brodkin 1998; Schraub 2019).

Still, there are a growing number of visible minority Jews. Some are of Sephardic/Middle Eastern origin, others Ethiopian, and others a result of mixed marriages or adoption. Jews are also both a religious group and an ethnic group and are recognized as such by the Canadian census. This means there are multiple points of potential divergence from mainstream society along religious and ethno-cultural lines. And the Jewish religion is itself highly diverse. In fact, ultra-Orthodox Jews. such as Hasidic Jews, can perhaps qualify as a "visible minority" because of their distinctive attire, and thus are more easily targeted for physical assault.

Because of the long Jewish diasporic tradition, antisemitism in its international manifestations, mainly in the United States and Europe, shapes Canadian Jewish perceptions as well. An ancient rabbinic saying claims that all Jews are linked, and the *Canadian Jewish News* features regular coverage of antisemitic incidents worldwide. Many Canadian Jews also follow such events in international Jewish online publications, such as the Jewish Telegraphic Agency (JTA), the *Forward*, or English editions of Israeli newspapers. Thus, measuring the perception of antisemitism by Canadian Jews should ideally include an international dimension, not usually captured by specifically Canadian indicators. To be blunt, when Jews are murdered in the streets of Europe or while praying in an American synagogue, it resonates in Canadian Jewish life, just as mass murders in mosques or Black churches resonate with worldwide Muslim and African-American communities. That is part of the reason why Canadian synagogues and communal institutions have recently heightened security measures (Lungen 2019).

When pondering the future evolution and impact of antisemitism in Canada, one should realize that predictions based only on survey data are fraught. Other sorts of information are worth considering as well. In the United States, the Southern Poverty Law Center has monitored growth in the number of extremist and militant groups from 457 in 1999 to 1,020 in 2018 (The Southern Poverty Law Center, 2019). People from these groups chanted "Jews will not replace us" in the 2017 Charlottesville "Unite the Right" rally. Most of these hate groups included antisemitism in their ideologies, along with racism, xenophobia, Islamophobia, populism, nationalism and fundamentalist Christianity. Of course, similar parties and movements have proliferated in Europe, in some cases seeming to re-open "the Jewish question" of previous generations. In Canada, the government has taken note of the rise of right-wing extremist groups as well as the spread of extremism in the ranks of the Canadian army (Canadian Jewish News Staff 2019; Farber 2019). The danger here is not simply occasional acts of violence, but the spread of accompanying exclusionary ideologies, proliferating in political parties such as the People's Party of Canada.

Up through the 1960s, one could argue that antisemitism was the dominant fact of North American Jewish life. For the next three to four decades, concern for antisemitism among scholars of North

American Jewry declined, and a focus on assimilation and intermarriage gained ground. In recent decades, antisemitism, often linked to expressions of anti-Israel sentiment and right-wing populism, has re-emerged on the Canadian Jewish communal agenda and in the private concerns of Canadian Jews.

I used to ask Jewish students at McGill University to recount experiences of antisemitism. Almost none of the students had been assaulted, been given a lower grade in school, been denied a job or paid lower wages, been denied accommodation or service, been harassed by police officers or store salespersons, or had their property vandalized or defaced. Nonetheless, most of them felt sincerely that they were real or potential victims. Jewish students, like other minority students, also claim to be affected by micro-aggressions: indirect, subtle or unintentional prejudice or discrimination (often verbal) against members of a marginalized group (Fleras 2016). More recently, some Jewish students have felt highly stressed and victimized as Jews by Israeli Apartheid and Boycott, Divestment, and Sanctions (BDS) campaigns on campus (Saxe et al. 2015).

By conventional measures, antisemitism in Canada today is far lower than in the immediate post-World War II period. Into the 1960s, quotas, formal or informal, still operated in universities and corporate boardrooms. An effective legal structure in dealing with human rights, non-discrimination and expressions of hate did not exist. Negative and demeaning stereotypes about Jews were widespread in all segments of the Canadian public. Jews faced discrimination in employment, accommodation and housing. Jewish children in public schools were usually expected to take part in all manner of Christian rituals and prayer. There were no human rights acts or human rights commissions, no hate literature laws, no constitutional protections. Jewish Holocaust survivors still had to overcome resistance to enter Canada after the war (Abella and Troper 1983; Robinson 2015).

Jews lived in a profoundly Jewish solitude, for reasons of choice and reasons of exclusion. *Crestwood Heights,* the pioneering study of Forest Hill in Toronto, described hesitant Jewish interactions with the majority non-Jewish population. Canadian Jews in the 1950s played down their Jewish identity, still insecure in their new-found middle-class suburban status (Seeley et al. 1956; Kallen 1977). The all-time best-selling book on a Canadian Jewish topic is *None Is Too Many,* exploring the antisemitism that provided the context of Canada's closed-door policy toward Jewish refugees before and during World War II (Abella and Troper 1983).

These exclusions notwithstanding, Canadian Jews have not suffered enormously from antisemitism. There have been no forced conversions, expulsions, pogroms, Dreyfus affairs, Nuremberg Laws or crematoria in this country. The antisemitism of Social Credit in Alberta, like that of American populism, remained on the fringe geographically and politically. Jews were never the absolute *others* as they were in Europe and occasionally in Arab/Muslim countries. French-English polarization and the victimization of First Nations and non-white minorities assured Jews a margin of acceptability and buffered the hatred. Canadian Jews have not been murdered by antisemites, as happened in the United States in notorious cases like the 1915 lynching of Leo Frank or the recent murders of Jews in their neighbourhoods and synagogues (Oney 2004). Yet this assessment of the relative advantage of the Canadian case does not obscure the universal sense of Jewish insecurity, captured in countless Jewish quips. ("If everything is so good, why is everything so bad?" "You know the difference between a Jewish optimist and a Jewish pessimist? The Jewish pessimist says, 'Things can't get any worse.' The Jewish optimist says, 'Yes they can.'")

Antisemitism in Canada dates back to before Confederation. It was found in both the French and English communities. Conflict over the 1807 election of Ezekiel Hart to the Legislative Assembly of Lower Canada included elements of antisemitism. Indeed, a theological antisemitism existed throughout the pre-Confederation era, even in the near absence of Jews (Menkis 1992; Robinson 2015). In French Canada, a steady stream of antisemitic thought was present, some homegrown and some imported from France (Brown 1992).

In English Canada, theological antisemitism was expressed in evangelical and missionary activity aimed at converting Jews and supporting such efforts elsewhere (Menkis 1992: 26–27). English Canada also developed a brand of "intellectual" antisemitism, typified by the writings of Goldwin Smith in the late nineteenth century (Tulchinsky 1992). Anglo antisemitism of this type helped feed into discrimination at Canadian universities. Jewish enrollment at McGill University declined between 1925 and 1935 from 25 to 12 per cent of the student population, and a Jewish quota at the University of Toronto Medical School was in place until 1959 (Anctil 1992; Levi 2003).

Canadian antisemitism reached its peak in the 1930s. Fascist organizations existed in both English and French Canada. In English Canada, antisemitism fed off Anglo-Saxon nativism and unemployment. The 1930s saw the development of swastika clubs and associations. The swastika figured in the largest Jewish-Gentile riot in Canadian history, which broke out in 1933 in Toronto's Christie Pits after a baseball game between a largely Jewish team and an Anglo-Saxon club (Levitt and Shaffir 1987).

In Quebec, the situation was more serious. Opposition to conscription in 1942 helped fuel traditional antisemitic currents, and vice versa. In the inter-war period, French nationalism embraced three themes, all of which fed antisemitism: re-francization, with Jews being identified with the English; promoting French entrepreneurs through the *achat chez nous* movement, which involved boycotting Jewish firms; and anti-immigration sentiment (Anctil 1992: 156). The conservative Catholic Church in Quebec opposed liberal and radical tendencies identified with Jews at home and abroad. Even more pronounced was the steady antisemitism in articles, letters and columns published in the influential *Le Devoir* (Abella 1990: 180; Anctil 1992: 148).

Adrien Arcand formed the National Social Christian Party on a Nazi model in 1934. To be sure, Arcand's movement numbered only in the hundreds. It petered out in the course of the war. But the fact that over 80 percent of Quebec voters, and more among francophones, rejected the possibility of conscription in the referendum in the spring of 1942 is revealing. In 1998, Esther Delisle's second book dealing with antisemitism and Nazi sympathizers in the post-war period, was, like her first book, greeted with a blend of silence and contempt (Delisle 1998). The contrast with the *mea culpas* and enthusiastic reception in English Canada of Irving Abella and Harold Troper's *None Is Too Many* is stark. In any case, after the war, organized political antisemitism was largely discredited.

Types of antisemitism

There are different ways of defining and measuring antisemitism. *De jure* antisemitism can be defined as being explicitly mandated in, or permitted by, legislation, or so interpreted by the courts. The British North America Act itself contains a form of legal discrimination against Jews and other religious minorities in the area of educational rights. Protestants and Catholics enjoy educational rights to state funding unavailable to Jews and other religious minorities. (Some provinces, though not Ontario, with around 60 percent of Canada's Jewish population, now partially fund Jewish schools.)

However, by and large, the force of law and jurisprudence in Canada today protects Jews (and other minorities) from discrimination and is a major impediment to antisemitism. This situation is typified by the adoption of the non-discriminatory immigration "points system" and the enactment of human rights legislation at provincial and federal levels. Nevertheless, there remain cases where law, or the interpretation of law, can harm Jewish interests. Quebec's Bill 21, passed in June 2019, curtails visible religious symbols in certain professions. It therefore limits career opportunities for kippah-wearing Jews, among others. As of this writing, the law is being challenged in court.

De facto antisemitism consists of acts by individual Canadians or institutions that may or may not be illegal but which harm Jews or hurt Jewish sensibilities. Some of these acts are motivated by anti-Jewish feeling, like an employer choosing not to hire a Jew. Others may be unintentional and simply have harmful consequences, like scheduling university exams on Passover.

Overt acts of antisemitism come in many forms. Acts of serious personal violence are rare in Canada. Defacement of property or general vandalism is more common. Overt or covert discrimination in employment or in any other public domain is also rare. Spoken insults or Internet postings such as those relating to Holocaust denial are another form of antisemitism, the latter of which have become all too common with the flowering of social media. Casual private comments or expressions can reflect prejudicial attitudes and are often offensive and hurtful to Jews. These can reflect stereotypes based on ignorance or malice, and some may not be intentionally hurtful. Many Jews see antisemitism as the subtext in criticism of Israel and Zionism (Brackman 2015).

Studies of racism in Canada and elsewhere almost never focus on the attitudes of minorities toward majorities. This is certainly true regarding Jews. Yet some Jews undeniably hold negative stereotypes about non-Jews. It is possible that the high level of Jewish residential segregation in Canada is based partly on such sentiment, as it is for some other middle-class minority groups (Harold and Fong 2018). It is also possible that residential mixing, like other forms of contact, is associated with lower levels of antisemitism. In 2009, 45 percent of Canadians reported having Jewish friends, ranging from a high of 61 percent in Ontario to a low of 20 per cent in Quebec (Geddes 2009). It is possible that the higher level of antisemitism among francophones, established in multiple surveys, may reflect a lack of contact (Brym and Lenton 1992).

Finally, antisemitism can permeate high culture and popular culture. Historically, this began as anti-Judaism, and included the theological conviction that Jews were *collectively* responsible for kill-ing Christ or that Judaism posed a threat to Christianity. Beyond that, it includes demeaning images of Jews in literature, intellectual discourse and daily language, or the absence of Jewish themes in Canadian cultural production. The images of Shylock or of rapacious Jewish businessmen or the use of "Jew" as a verb are well-known examples. This type of cultural antisemitism was more prevalent in the past, in both English and French Canada.

The thematic content of traditional explicit antisemitism in the West can be reduced to four broad types (Wistrich 2010). First, religious *Christian antisemitism* feeds on the Christ-killer theme. More recent elements of theological anti-Judaism found in some fundamentalist Christian denominations carry on this tradition. A second type is *racist antisemitism*, rooted in biology, not belief. Proponents of this view argue that Jews are non-human, sub-human or at the very least racially distinct from Aryans or non-Jews. Racist antisemitism also relates to Jews as a people or ethnic group with certain negative stereotypical traits.

Then there are two types of political or economic antisemitism. *Right-wing antisemitism* opposes Jews because they are seen to support liberalism, socialism or communism. More recently, Jews have earned the enmity of the religious right by being identified with liberal or progressive positions—pro-choice, pro-sex education, pro-gay rights. *Left-wing antisemitism* opposes Jews because they are seen as arch-capitalists, greedy exploiters of the working class, devoted to moneymaking and material pursuits. This strain goes back to the Middle Ages, when the image of the Jew as usurer or moneylender was widespread. A controversial recent variant attacks Zionism as reactionary nationalism, with Israel and its Jewish supporters an extension of Western imperialism aimed at oppressing Arabs.

How can Jews be, at the same time, a religious group and a racial group, communists and capitalists, freethinkers and ultra-Orthodox? The myth of a Jewish conspiracy resolves all these contradictions. The *Protocols of the Elders of Zion,* fabricated by the Tsarist Secret police in the early 20th century, is the modern foundational document (Cohn 1967). It portrays all types of Jews as part of one overarching conspiracy, aided by the alleged Jewish control of the media, aimed at world domination (Hitler 1943).

The shadow of the Holocaust looms over Canadian Jewry, shaping attitudes about antisemitism. A 2018 survey found that 69 percent of Canadian Jews regard "remembering the Holocaust" as essential to being Jewish, second only to "leading an ethical and moral life" at 72 percent (Brym, Neuman and Lenton 2019: 18). In contrast, a 2019 survey discovered that one-fifth of Canadian young people had not heard of the Holocaust or were not sure what it was. Nearly two-thirds of the sample did not know or underestimated the numbers of Jews killed (Arsenault 2019). Holocaust ignorance resurfaced during the 2015 federal election campaign. Alex Johnstone, an NDP candidate from Ontario and a long-time school trustee and public-school official, admitted that she was unfamiliar with the fact that Auschwitz was a World War II death camp (Maloney 2015).

Two Canadian Holocaust denial cases in the 1980s were well publicized. Ernst Zündel was a German-born publisher of materials denying the Holocaust and preaching a Jewish international conspiracy for world domination. He was prosecuted under an obscure Criminal Code provision against the spreading of false news. He was eventually deported to Germany where he was convicted of Holocaust denial in 2007. Jim Keegstra was a social studies teacher in Eckville, Alberta. He was initially prosecuted in 1985 under the hate literature laws in the Criminal Code for "willfully promoting hatred" against the Jewish people. He taught his high-school students that the major events of Western history were largely the result of an international Jewish conspiracy (Bercuson and Wertheimer 1985; Mertl and Ward 1985). The case eventually wound up in the Supreme Court, which upheld the constitutionality of the hate speech laws as a legitimate restriction of free speech under Section One of the Charter of Rights and Freedoms.

The tension between the right of free speech and hate speech will likely never be resolved (Lipstadt 1993). New cases with slightly different twists in new jurisdictions, will arise. Hate messages on the Internet and on social media are a troubling new version (Lungen 2016). Canada's hate speech laws in the Criminal Code and in provincial statutes recognize that absolutes are rare, and that more often principles will jostle one another. When that happens, the courts must sort things out. Depending on how courts adjudicate such cases, Canada's commitment to restrictions on hate speech, while troubling for civil libertarians, is an impediment to the growth of antisemitism.

Data on Canadian antisemitism

Canadian incidents of extreme antisemitism are now rare, but they could happen. Consider a hypothetical free speech issue relating to Israel. In its most extreme form, anti-Zionism opposes the right of Jews to a state of their own. Given that 6.7 million Jews now live in such a state and defend its existence tooth and nail, denying the existential right of a Jewish state is for most Jews unambiguous antisemitism. A free-speech court case could easily take place over this issue.

What about opposition to one or more Israeli *policies*? This is a more complex issue. Some Jews consider anti-Zionism to be distinct from antisemitism and claim that the charge of antisemitism is often used by pro-Israel supporters to shield Israel from legitimate criticism. In 2020, when Israeli Prime Minister Binyamin Netanyahu endorsed Donald Trump's "Deal of the Century" sanctioning the annexation of most of the West Bank by Israel, a public opinion poll revealed that 45 percent of Israelis oppose *any* annexation (Gross 2020). Jews who distinguish anti-Zionism from antisemitism might argue that these results hardly justify the view that nearly half of Israelis are antisemites. Nonetheless, as overt antisemitism has become unfashionable, many Jews have come to consider any criticism of Israel a convenient substitute for antisemitism (Fulford 2018).

This issue is hotly debated in the Canadian Jewish community. In 2016, a conservative American Jewish newspaper, *The Algemeiner*, published a list of the 40 most hostile North American campuses for Jewish students. The University of Toronto ranked number three, McGill University number four (*The Algemeiner* 2016). Most of the incidents counted in the study involved anti-Israel activity. For example, at McGill University they included multiple attempts to pass BDS resolutions, the prohibition of pro-Israel newspaper articles and a notorious tweet by a Jewish student involved in student government urging his colleagues to "punch a Zionist" (Fegelman 2015; Harrison 2006; Levitan 2015; Taguieff 2001: 12–13).

One prominent source of data on antisemitism in Canada is the annual report on antisemitic incidents of the League for Human Rights of B'nai Brith Canada. The number of incidents reported for 2018 was 2,041, compared 1,269 for 2015 and to 240 for 1998. Of the 2018 incidents, 1,809 involved harassment, 221 vandalism, and 11 personal violence. Much of the increase comes from more effective collection procedures. There has also been an explosion of antisemitic comments online, with a single tweet now counting as an incident (Brym 2019). Still, one should not conclude that impactful antisemitism has increased nine-fold over the past 20 years, as B'nai Brith Canada data claim ("B'nai Brith Audit Reveals Anti-Semitism In Canada Reaches An All-Time High" 2015; B'nai Brith Canada 2019).

What sorts of incidents are these? The following descriptions from the 2018 B'nai Brith report gives us a sense of the range: While treating a patient crying from severe sinus pain, an ER nurse in Ontario calls the patient "a spoiled rich Jewish [expletive] just looking for free meds." Graffiti reading "Kill the Jews" with a swastika was drawn on a bus stop in Kirkland, Quebec. Four religious Jewish teenagers are out for a walk in Toronto were verbally abused and physically attacked by a group of teenagers (B'nai Brith Canada 2019).

Data on antisemitic acts are also available from official law enforcement records. A 2010 report on law enforcement studies in Canada and the U.S. found that Jews were "overwhelmingly and disproportionately" the target of hate crimes when compared with other religious minorities (B'nai Brith Canada 2010). The Statistics Canada police-reported hate crime report for 2017 found that Jews were the most targeted of all minority groups, with 360 reported incidents. The Muslim community's police reported hate crimes were second at 349 incidents (Statistics Canada 2018). Given that the Muslim Canadian population is three times larger than the Jewish Canadian population, the hate crime rate is about three times higher for Jews. Police data for hate crimes in Toronto found a similar pattern. Jews comprised 38 percent of victimized groups, followed by Muslims, with Blacks at about 15 percent (Toronto Police Service 2018). Part of this Jewish-Muslim gap may be due to reporting bias, in that Muslim Canadians are more likely to be immigrants and therefore might feel less comfortable about reporting such attacks.

A 2015 survey of American and Canadian Jewish university students examined "the extent of hostility toward Israel and antisemitism on North American campuses" (Saxe et al. 2015). It found that Canadian universities were overrepresented in the high hostility group (Saxe et al. 2015). Of course, many BDS supporters claim that they are in no way antisemitic and only oppose Israeli policies, and while that is probably true for some supporters, it is probably not true for all of them. Thus, at McGill University in 2016, a BDS motion was passed at a student union meeting but then rejected in an online ratification vote. Jewish students reported increasing tension on campus, exemplified by a statement found on a social media site claiming that "Little Zionist Jewboys [are] not happy that McGill students don't support their genocide" (Seidman 2016).

Does all this amount to a "great deal" of antisemitism? Obviously, perceptions are shaped by media reporting of individual incidents, so the extent of bigotry is inevitably multiplied. Yet both the League for Human Rights and police services claim that reported incidents represent 10 per cent of all cases. Each one can hurt dozens or thousands of Jews, depending on the degree of publicity.

Jewish Canadians do not seem to be penalized in terms of educational, occupational and income attainment. This outcome does not prove the absence of antisemitism in the workplace, since it is possible that Jewish attainment (like the attainment of certain Asian groups) can take place despite discrimination. Many Jews find employment in Jewish-owned firms or institutions, thus joining the Jewish "sub-economy," while many others are self-employed, mitigating the impact of work-related antisemitism (Weinfeld, Schnoor and Shames 2018: 218–41).

Antisemitic prejudice and Jewish/non-Jewish interactions

How extensive are antisemitic attitudes in Canada, and where are they concentrated? About 43 per cent of American Jews, compared with 24 per cent of the American public, felt that "there is a lot of discrimination against Jews" (Pew Research Center 2013: 105). In Canada in 2018, 34 percent of Jews felt there was discrimination against Jews "often" (51 percent felt Muslims were similarly victimized). When asked about personal experiences of discrimination, 21 percent reported such experience due to their religion, and 18 percent due to ethnicity or culture. These levels were roughly similar in Montreal and Toronto, and for Canadian Muslims compared to Canadian Jews (Brym, Neuman and Lenton 2019: 47–55).

How do these perceptions compare with Canadian popular attitudes? A 2008 poll found that 13 percent of Canadians had an "unfavourable opinion" of Jews—7 percent in English Canada and 27 percent in Quebec. In comparison, 7 percent of Americans and 9 percent of British respondents had unfavourable opinions of Jews. Notably, 36 percent of Canadians had an unfavourable opinion of Muslims (33 percent in English Canada and 49 percent in French Canada) (Jedwab 2008). A 2009 survey found that 72 percent of Canadians had a positive view of Christianity, 53 percent of Judaism and 28 percent of Islam. Respondents in Ontario were the most favorable towards Judaism at 59 percent, while those from Quebec were least favourable at 36 percent (Geddes 2009). A 2014 survey of international antisemitism by the Anti-Defamation League used an 11-item index to measure antisemitism. Respondents who answered "true or probably true" to any six of the following eleven items were labelled antisemitic:

1. Jews are more loyal to Israel than to [this country/the countries they live in].
2. Jews have too much power in international financial markets.

3. Jews have too much control over global affairs.
4. Jews think they are better than other people.
5. Jews have too much control over the global media.
6. Jews are responsible for most of the world's wars.
7. Jews have too much power in the business world.
8. Jews don't care what happens to anyone but their own kind.
9. People hate Jews because of the way Jews behave.
10. Jews have too much control over the United States government.
11. Jews still talk too much about what happened to them in the Holocaust.

The survey found a 14 percent antisemitic index score for Canada. This compares with 9 percent for the US, 8 percent for Britain, 5 percent for the Netherlands, 27 percent for Germany and 37 percent for France. According to the survey, 23 percent of Canadians believe Jews have too much power in the business world and international financial markets, and 18 percent believe Jews hold too much control over global media (Anti-Defamation League 2014). Distrusting Jews in positions of political power, as seen in the ADL items, is another common indicator of antisemitism. Mistrust might relate to the representation of Jews in elected office. After the 2015 Canadian elections, 1.7 percent of MPs were Jewish, just above the population proportion of 1.2 percent. In the US, the UK, and France, elected proportions are much higher than population proportions (Weinfeld 2020).

Another study found that religiosity is no longer a source of antisemitism; those who believed that a "Christian commitment was needed for salvation" were not more apt to be anti-Jewish (Weimann and Winn 1986: 144). Contact with Jews also plays a role. Canadians who have met at least one Jew are less likely to be prejudiced than those who have met none. A 2009 survey found that 76 per cent of Canadians with Jewish friends were favorably disposed toward Judaism, while only 34 per cent of people with no Jewish friends had a favourable opinion of Judaism (Geddes 2009). Of course, it is not clear what is cause and what is effect here.

It is hard to interpret the importance of survey questions when they focus on attitudes rather than actual behaviors. Consider intermarriage, which can be seen as a sign of non-Jewish acceptance. From 1975 to 1995, there was a clear increase by Canadians in the approval of Jewish-non-Jewish marriages (Bibby 1995). A 2009 survey found that Judaism ranks only behind Christianity as an acceptable religion for the children of Canadians who would intermarry; 56 per cent claimed it was acceptable for their child to marry a Jew (Geddes 2009). In terms of actual intermarriage rates, about 77 percent of Canadian Jews in 2018 had a spouse who was Jewish by religion, with the level somewhat higher for older Canadians (Brym, Neuman and Lenton 2019: 39–40, 45).

As noted, negative attitudes toward Israel and/or Zionism have emerged as perhaps the major new focus of real or perceived antisemitism. This was the perception of many British Jews regarding Jeremy Corbyn and the Labour party. However, the link between antisemitism and opposition to Zionism, to Israel's right to exist as a Jewish state, or to Israeli policies, is not clear cut, and highly contentious in general political discourse as well as among Jews (Brym 2019).

On the one hand, harsh criticism of Israeli policies would in theory not qualify as antisemitism, though some supporters of Israel might feel that double standard criticism, or highly intensive criticism, might have antisemitic overtones. And some on-campus incidents in Canada have conflated the two (Brym 2019: 411–12). But it is likely that for many or most diaspora Jews, very harsh criticism of Israel veers into antisemitism. Thus, 34 percent of Canadian Jews report having been criticized for defending Israeli policies or actions of Israel, and 31 percent (likely very overlapping) have refrained from expressing support for Israel (Brym, Neuman and Lenton, 2019: 53).

Social scientists have measured the correlation between anti-Israel attitudes and antisemitic attitudes. While there has been little research on this subject in Canada, a major British survey found that "even harsh criticism of Israel was not necessarily antisemitic, but harsh criticism of Israel was likely to be associated with some level of antisemitism, in some cases a high level" (Brym 2019: 416).

In addition to findings of survey research, major organizations of the Canadian Jewish community such as B'nai Brith, as well as the Canadian Parliamentary Coalition to Combat Antisemitism, argue that many of the incidents on the ground justify conflation of antisemitism and anti-Israel motivations (Brym 2019: 411). Indeed, Canadian Jewish organizations, as well as the Canadian Parliament, have adopted a definition of antisemitism developed by the International Holocaust Remembrance Association that includes elements of anti-Zionism or anti-Israelism. The definition was adopted by Canada's Parliament in 2019 but was met with criticism by elements of the NDP, civil liberties associations, and the BDS-supporting Independent Jewish Voices, which feared the definition would work to suppress criticism of Israel and limit free speech (Maura 2019). Among the elements of the definition that refer to Israel are "denying the Jewish people their right to self determination, e.g. by claiming that the existence of a State of Israel is a racist endeavour," or "applying double standards by requiring of [Israel] a behaviour not expected or demanded of any other democratic nation" (B'nai Brith Canada 2019: 8).

Canadian Jews pay attention to political party support for Israel. About one quarter of the 12 percent of Jewish supporters of the NDP and Green party feel that Canada is too supportive of Israel; this is true for only three percent of the supporters of the Liberals and Conservatives, who represent 68 percent of Canadian Jewish voters. Among Conservative Jewish supporters, many of whom recall the Harper government fondly, 60 percent find the Canadian government "not supportive enough." This is true for only 26 percent of Liberal supporters. These findings reflect the emergence of support for Israel as a wedge political issue in the Jewish community. It dates back to the turn of the century, as some prominent Jewish Liberal supporters moved to support the Harper Conservatives, who seemed more committed to Israel than the Liberals were (Barry 2010; Brym, Neuman and Lenton 2019; Weinfeld, Schnoor and Shames 2018: 245–7).

Intersectionality and reciprocal solidarity play an important role in the make-up of contemporary antisemitism and anti-Zionism among liberal and progressive elements. A prominent case is the way in which feminist groups and causes, including some in Canada, have attempted to vilify and exclude Jewish or Zionist women or from events such as Gay pride parades. Opponents of Israel reject "pink-washing", that is, using relatively liberal attitudes towards LGBTQ individuals found in gay-friendly cities such as Tel Aviv to excuse or distract from Israeli mistreatment of Palestinians (Weinfeld, Schnoor and Shames 2018: 140). More recently, intersectionality via BDS has extended into veganism. In 2019, a group called "Vegans for BDS" organized a panel discussion on the University of Toronto campus called "No Veganwashing Israeli crimes." Speakers challenged the authenticity of Israel's vegan movement and voiced support for Palestine's animal rights movement (Fraiman 2019).

The Jewish case likely parallels similar developments for other

Canadian minority groups with diasporic ties. The ease and relatively low cost of international travel and communication strengthens diaspora-homeland ties for many minorities (Satzewich and Wong 2006). Multicultural policy has a similar effect. While loyalty to a homeland does not necessarily challenge loyalty to Canada (Satzewich 2007), it may be seen as leading to possible foreign policy challenges; some minority groups who oppose Canadian government foreign policy or seek to change it could be seen as suspect or disloyal (Granatstein 2008). Jews have certainly long wrestled with the canard of dual loyalty (Weinfeld 2015). This sentiment could fuel racism, as it has in the past, notably with the forced relocation of Japanese Canadians during World War II (Adachi 1991). In short, disagreements on foreign policy issues may became more salient in shaping domestic Canadian ethnic relations, including relations between Canadian Jews and Muslims.

Finally, antisemitism in Quebec has had and still has a distinctive edge. In Quebec today, antisemitism is more than the residue of staunch Catholicism. Jews in Quebec are overwhelmingly federalists and are perceived as such by Quebec nationalists and *independentistes*. In a 2007 poll, 41 percent of French speakers in the province agreed with the statement, "Jews want to impose their customs and traditions on others," while just 31 percent agreed that "Jews want to participate fully in society" (Robinson 2013). Jacques Parizeau's attack against "money and the ethnic vote" after the 1995 referendum defeat jarred many Jews. While Parti Québécois leaders have generally opposed antisemitism, most Jews fear Québécois nationalism.

Historically, the level of antisemitic attitudes in the general population has been higher in *la belle province* than elsewhere in Canada. It hardly helped matters when, in 1990, Pierre Péladeau, a prominent Quebec businessman and father of former Parti Québécois leader Pierre Karl Péladeau, told a Quebec newsmagazine that he has great respect for Jews, but "they take up too much space" (Littman 1991). More recently, in 2014, the well-known Quebec radio host Gilles Proulx stated on air that Jews manipulated world governments and took economic control of the countries in which they lived, and Louise Mailloux, a PQ candidate, publicly expressed her belief that kosher food is a scam and that its proceeds may be funding religious wars (Robinson 2013).

Policy

How do we understand the fact that many Canadian Jews believe themselves to be potential victims without having actually been seriously victimized? An ideology of omnipresent antisemitism is part of modern Jewish identity. It explains the enduring potency of the Holocaust as an image for Jews far removed from the death camps in Europe, which permeates Canadian Jewish life (Harold 2020; Harold and Fong 2018). It also explains why concern for the fate of Israel remains important, even as Israel appears militarily strong, and thus why apparent opposition to Israel's existence as a secure and Jewish state resonates for many Jews as antisemitic. These insecurities persist despite the fact that, on most measures, Canadian Jews are relatively affluent and seemingly well integrated socially and culturally.

What can be done to reduce the level of antisemitism in Canada? First, increased collaboration is needed between Jews and other victimized groups, as in the case of liaisons with Muslims and Sikhs in opposition to Quebec's Bill 21. Second, efforts must be taken to eliminate hateful elements in public discourse while retaining commitment to freedom of speech. Universities would be an important locus of attention in this regard. Another would involve increased regulation of racist internet sites. Third, governments and NGOs need to initiate programs to increase social interaction between Jewish and non-Jewish groups. In general, a national service program for Canadian youth might help to break down barriers among all Canadian ethnic, racial and religious groups. Fourth, and perhaps most difficult, government should try to shape a national discourse recognizing that ties between diasporas and their homelands are an important and non-threatening part of Canada's strong multicultural fabric.

References

Abella, I. 1990. *A Coat of Many Colours: Two Centuries of Jewish Life in Canada*. Lester and Orpen Dennys.

Abella, I. and Troper, H. M. 1983. *None is Too Many: Canada and the Jews of Europe, 1933–1948*. Lester and Orpen Dennys.

Adachi, K. 1991. *The Enemy That Never Was: A History of the Japanese Canadians*, 2nd ed. McClelland and Stewart, in association with the Multiculturalism Department of the Secretary of State of Canada.

Anctil, P. 1992. Interlude of hostility: Judeo-Christian relations in Quebec in the inter-war period, 1919–1939. Pp. 135–66 in A. Davies Ed., *Anti-Semitism in Canada: History and Interpretation* Waterloo: Wilfred Laurier University Press.

Anti-Defamation League. 2014. *ADL Global 100: 2014 Survey Results*. ADL Global 100. https://global100.adl.org/map.

Arsenault, C. 2019. 1 in 5 Canadian youths not sure what happened in the Holocaust, survey suggests. *CBC News*, 27 January. https://www.cbc.ca/news/canada/canada-holocaust-survey-remembrance-1.4994602.

Barry, D. 2010. Canada and the Middle East today: electoral politics and foreign policy. *Arab Studies Quarterly* 32(4): 191–217.

Bercuson, D. J. and Wertheimer, D. 1985. *A Trust Betrayed: The Keegstra Affair*. Toronto: Doubleday Canada.

Bibby, R. W. 1995. *The Bibby Report: Social Trends Canadian Style*. Toronto: Stoddart Publishing.

B'nai Brith Audit Reveals Anti-Semitism In Canada Reaches An All-Time High. 2015, June 11. *Edmonton Jewish News*. https://www.edmonton-jewishnews.com/bnai-brith-canada-releases-2014-audit-of-anti-semitic-incidents-in-canada/.

B'nai Brith Canada. 2010. *2009 Audit of Antisemitic Incidents*. Toronto: League for Human Rights of B'nai Brith Canada.

B'nai Brith Canada. 2019. *2018 Annual Audit of Antisemitic Incidents*. Toronto: League for Human Rights of B'nai Brith Canada. https://www.bnaibrith.ca/a_new_normal_antisemitism_in_canada_sets_record_for_third_consecutive_year.

Brackman, H. 2015. Regents beware: You are already under attack for calling out 'anti-Zionism'. *Jewish Journal*, 11 June. https://jewishjournal.com/blogs/brackmans-history-matters/174453/.

Brodkin, K. 1998. *How Jews Became White Folks and What That Says About Race in America*. New Brunswick, NJ: Rutgers University Press.

Brown, M. 1992. From stereotype to scapegoat: anti-Jewish sentiment in French Canada from Confederation to World War One. Pp. 239–66 in A. Davies, ed., *Anti-Semitism in Canada: History and Interpretation*. Waterloo: Wilfred Laurier University Press.

Brym, R. 2019. Antisemitic and anti-Israel actions and attitudes in Canada and internationally: a research agenda. *Patterns of Prejudice* 53(4): 407–20.

Brym, R. and Lenton, R. 1991. The distribution of anti-Semitism in Canada in 1984. *Canadian Journal of Sociology/Cahiers Canadiens de Sociologie* 16(4): 411–18.

Brym, R. and Lenton, R. 1992. Anti-Semitism in Quebec. *Canadian Journal of Sociology/ Cahiers Canadiens de Sociologie* 17(2): 179–83.

Brym, R., Neuman, K. and Lenton, R. 2019. *2018 Survey of Jews in Canada: Final Report.* Toronto: Environics Institute. https://www.environicsinstitute.org/docs/default-source/project-documents/2018-survey-of-jews-in-canada/2018-survey-of-jews-in-canada---final-report.pdf?sfvrsn=2994ef6_2.

Canadian Jewish News Staff. 2019. Canada adds neo-Nazi, Iran-Backed Groups to Terrorist Watch List. *Canadian Jewish News*, 27 June. https://www.cjnews.com/news/canada/canada-adds-neo-nazi-iran-backed-groups-to-terrorist-watch-list.

Cohn, N. 1967. *Warrant for Genocide: The Myth of the Jewish World-Conspiracy and the Protocols of the Elders of Zion.* New York: Harper and Row.

Delisle, E. 1998. *Myths, Memory and Lies: Quebec's Intelligentsia and the Fascist Temptation, 1939–1960.* Montreal: Robert Davies Multimedia.

Farber, B. 2019. Extremists in our ranks. *Canadian Jewish News*, 27 June. https://www.cjnews.com/perspectives/opinions/farber-extremists-in-our-ranks.

Fegelman, M. 2015. When criticism of Israel becomes Anti-Semitism. *Huffington Post*, August 31. https://www.huffingtonpost.ca/mike-fegelman/criticism-of-israel_b_8050548.html.

Fleras, A. 2016. Theorizing Micro-aggressions as racism 3.0: shifting the discourse. *Canadian Ethnic Studies*, 48(2): 1–19. https://doi.org/10.1353/ces.2016.0011.

Fraiman, M. 2019. Rise of the vegan Jew. *Canadian Jewish News*, 2 October. https://www.cjnews.com/food/rise-of-the-vegan-jew.

Fulford, R. 2018. The BDS movement, where the anti-Semites find room to flourish. *National Post*, 30 November. https://nationalpost.com/opinion/robert-fulford-the-bds-movement-where-the-anti-semites-find-room-to-flourish.

Geddes, J. 2009. What Canadians think of Sikhs, Jews, Christians, Muslims... *Maclean's*, 28 April. https://www.macleans.ca/news/canada/what-canadians-think-of-sikhs-jews-christians-muslims/.

Granatstein, J. L. 2008. Multiculturalism and Canadian foreign policy. Pp. 78-91 in D. Bercuson and D. Carment, eds., *The World in Canada: Diaspora, Demography, and Domestic Politic.* Montreal and Kingston: McGill-Queen's University Press.

Gross, Judah Ari. 2020. Nearly half of Jewish Israelis oppose unilateral West Bank annexation – poll. *Times of Israel,* 29 January. https://www.timesofisrael.com/nearly-half-of-jewish-israelis-oppose-unilateral-west-bank-annexation-poll/.

Harold, J. 2020. *A Genesis of Jewishness: Collective Memory, Identity Work, and Collective Boundary Making Among Jews in Toronto.* PhD dissertation, Department of Sociology, University of Toronto.

Harold, J. and Fong, E. 2018. Mnemonic institutions and residential clustering: Jewish residential patterns in Toronto. *Canadian Review of Sociology/Revue Canadienne de Sociologie*, 55(2): 257–77.

Harrison, B. 2006. *The Resurgence of Anti-Semitism: Jews, Israel, and Liberal Opinion.* Lanham, MD: Rowman and Littlefield.

Hitler, A. 1943. *Mein Kampf,* R. Manheim, trans. Boston: Houghton Mifflin.

Jedwab, J. 2008. *Attitudes towards Jews and Muslims: Comparing Canada with the United States and Europe.* Association for Canadian Studies. http://ciim.ca/pdf/polls/12218487649334.pdf.

Kallen, E. 1977. *Spanning the Generations: A Study in Jewish Identity.* Toronto: Longman Canada.

Levi, C. 2003. There is a definite limitation imposed (Robin Ross to Claude Bissell, December 4, 1959): The Jewish Quota in the Faculty of Medicine, University of Toronto: Generational Memory Sustained by Documentation. *Historical Studies in Education/Revue d'histoire de l'éducation* 15(1): 131–8.

Levitan, T. 2015. Criticizing Israel's politics isn't anti-Semitism. *Huffington Post*, 14 August. https://www.huffingtonpost.ca/tyler-levitan/handling-of-antisemitism-_b_7984600.html.

Levitt, C. H. and Shaffir, W. 1987. *The Riot at Christie Pits.* Toronto: Lester and Orpen Dennys.

Lipstadt, D. E. 1993. *Denying the Holocaust: The Growing Assault on Truth and Memory.* New York: Free Press.

Littman, S. 1991. *Quebec's Jews: Vital Citizens or Eternal Strangers: Analysis of Key Newspaper Coverage of Three Pertinent Incidents.* Los Angeles and Toronto: Simon Wiesenthal Center.

Lowenstein, S. M. 2005. Jewish intermarriage and conversion in Germany and Austria. *Modern Judaism* 25(1): 23–61.

Lungen, P. 2016. B'nai Brith audit finds anti-Semitism moving online. *Canadian Jewish News*, 2 May. https://www.cjnews.com/news/canada/bnai-brith-audit-finds-anti-semitism-moving-online.

Lungen, P. 2019. Federal government giving $95k to Toronto shul for security upgrades. *Canadian Jewish News*, 28 August. https://www.cjnews.com/news/canada/federal-government-giving-95k-to-toronto-shul-for-security-upgrades.

Maloney, R. 2015. Alex Johnstone, NDP Candidate, Says She Didn't Know Auschwitz Was A Death Camp. *Huffington Post*, 23 September. https://www.huffingtonpost.ca/2015/09/23/alex-johnstone-ndp-auschwitz_n_8186098.html.

Maura, F. 2019. There's a debate over Canada's new definition of anti-Semitism, and it might sound strangely familiar. *National Post*, 27 June. https://nationalpost.com/news/politics/theres-a-debate-over-canadas-new-definition-of-anti-semitism-and-it-might-sound-strangely-familiar.

Menkis, R. 1992. Anti-Semitism and Anti-Judaism in Pre-Confederation

Canada. Pp. 11–38 in A. Davies, ed., *Anti-Semitism in Canada: History and Interpretation*. Waterloo: Wilfrid Laurier University Press.

Mertl, S. and Ward, J. 1985. *Keegstra: The Issues, the Trial, the Consequences*. Western Saskatoon: Producer Prairie Books.

Oney, S. 2004. *And the Dead Shall Rise: The Murder of Mary Phagan and the Lynching of Leo Frank*. New York: Vintage.

Pew Research Center. 2013. *A Portrait of Jewish Americans* Pew Research Center. https://www.pewresearch.org/wp-content/uploads/sites/7/2013/10/jewish-american-full-report-for-web.pdf.

Robinson, I. 2013. Reflections on antisemitism in French Canada. *Canadian Jewish Studies/Études Juives Canadienne*, 21(1): 90–122.

Satzewich, V. 2007. Multiculturalism, transnationalism, and the hijacking of Canadian foreign policy: a pseudo-problem? *International Journal*, 63(1): 43–62.

Satzewich, V. and Wong, L. L., eds. 2006. *Transnational Identities and Practices in Canada*. Vancouver: UBC Press.

Saxe, L., Sasson, T., Wright, G. and Hecht, S. 2015. *Antisemitism on the College Campus: Perceptions and Realities*. Brandeis University: Maurice and Marilyn Cohen Center for Modern Jewish Studies. https://bir.brandeis.edu/handle/10192/30810.

Schraub, D. 2019. White Jews: an intersectional approach. *Association for Jewish Studies Review*, 43(2): 379–407.

Seeley, J. R., Sim, R. A. and Loosley, E. W. 1956. *Crestwood Heights: A Study of the Culture of Suburban Life*. Toronto: University of Toronto Press.

Seidman, K. 2016. BDS vote stirs up hostilities on McGill campus. *Montreal Gazette*, 25 February. https://montrealgazette.com/news/local-news/bds-vote-stirs-up-hostilities-on-mcgill-campus.

Sklare, M. and Greenblum, J. 1967. *Jewish Identity on the Suburban Frontier: A Study of Group Survival in the Open Society*, vol. 1. New York: Basic Books.

The Southern Poverty Law Center. 2019. Hate by the numbers. *Rage against Change* 166: 39–42. https://www.splcenter.org/sites/default/files/intelligence_report_166.pdf.

Statistics Canada. 2018. *Police-Reported Hate Crime, 2017*. https://www150.statcan.gc.ca/n1/daily-quotidien/181129/dq181129a-eng.htm.

Taguieff, P.-A. 2001. *La nouvelle judéophobie*. Paris: Mille et une nuits.

The Algemeiner. 2016. The Algemeiner's 1st annual list of the US and Canada's worst campuses for Jewish Students. https://www.algemeiner.com/the-40-worst-colleges-for-jewish-students-2016/.

Toronto Police Service. 2018. *2018 Annual Hate Crime Statistical Report*. Toronto Police Service: Intelligence Services, Hate Crime Unit. http://www.torontopolice.on.ca/publications/files/reports/2018hatecrimereport.pdf.

Tulchinsky, G. 1992. Goldwin Smith: Victorian-Canadian anti-Semite. Pp. 67–92 in A. Davies, ed. *Anti-Semitism in Canada: History and Interpretation* Waterloo: Wilfred Laurier University Press.

Weimann, G. and Winn, C. 1986. *Hate on Trial: The Zundel Affair, the Media, and Public Opinion in Canada.* Toronto: Mosaic Press.

Weinfeld, M. 2015. Canadian Jews, dual/divided loyalties, and the Tebbit "Cricket" Test. Pp. 141–58 in S. Guoand L. Wong, eds., *Revisiting Multiculturalism in Canada: Theories, Policies, and Debates.* Rotterdam, Boston and Taipei: SensePublishers.

Weinfeld, M. 2020. Canadian Jews: A Comparative Perspective. In D. S. Koffman Ed., *No Better Home? Jews, Canada, and the Sense of Belonging.* Toronto: University of Toronto Press.

Weinfeld, M., Schnoor, R. F. and Shames, M. 2018. *Like Everyone Else, but Different: The Paradoxical Success of Canadian Jews,* 2nd ed. Montreal and Kingston: McGill-Queen's University Press.

Wistrich, R. S. 2010. *A Lethal Obsession: Anti-Semitism from Antiquity to the Global Jihad.* New York: Random House.

CHAPTER FIVE

Critical Notes on Racism, Islamophobia and Antisemitism

Neda Maghbouleh

Anti-Black racism, Islamophobia and antisemitism are typically studied separately. An inclusive approach that takes a comparative perspective and nudges us toward a politics of solidarity is a promising path forward out of present circumstances and into a more just and fair future. By providing historicized accounts of anti-Black racism, Islamophobia and antisemitism in Canada, each scholar in this volume has responded to the sociological vision of S.D. Clark, who cautioned that "only through an examination of [past] developments can an adequate theory of social change be formulated" (Clark 1948: vii). In this commentary, I briefly summarize each scholar's contribution before elaborating on steps we can take to remake our world in light of the barriers and challenges the panelists have identified.

Taken as a whole, the papers offer an informed evaluation of one aspect of the successes and failures of liberal democracy. On the negative side, and spanning different institutional and everyday spheres, they provide strong evidence of entrenched patterns of prejudice in Canada. The papers also raise questions of enduring importance: Who are the "fully human subjects" in the "imagined community" of Canada (Mills 1997; Anderson 1983)? Does "methodological nationalism," or an overemphasis on the nation, in this case Canada, impede us from understanding processes—violence, oppression and subjugation—that have no respect for borders (Wimmer and Glick Schiller 2003)? Previous sociological research has sought to identify groups whose members are denied full personhood and articulate the conditions under which this denial takes place. At times, this research has also overprivileged the nation as the appropriate unit of analysis. The papers in this volume engage the question of personhood by rigorously analyzing Canadian manifestations of transnational social ailments. Readers concerned with the future of Canadian society and the global future of human rights, social inclusion and mutual understanding will gain much from reading the papers.

Abdolmohammad Kazemipur provides sociohistorical context

for today's expressions of dehumanization, othering and violence against Muslim Canadians. He presents novel evidence of an association between Canada's contemporary reputation as a peacekeeping and humanitarian actor on the world stage and how the "Muslim question" was discussed mainly as a global security issue rather than a domestic problem in Canadian parliamentary debate through the 1990s and 2000s. Kazemipur highlights two narratives that pervade almost all conversations about Islamophobia in Canada: (1) Canada as a compassionate global actor with clean hands in the history of colonial dispossession in the Muslim world and (2) Canada as the exemplary case for how to build a multicultural mosaic of social harmony. Both narratives hinge on a notion of Canadian exceptionalism, assuming that things happening abroad do not affect Muslim and other minority faith communities here, and that white supremacist violence, murder and hate of Muslims here should be attributed to ideologies born elsewhere.

In his analysis, Kazemipur finds that Canadian political language about Muslims has recently shifted from framing Islam as a global threat that exists abroad toward a French or American style of suspicion, distrust and exclusion of a Muslim Canadian enemy within. While presenting evidence that questions standard Canadian political correctness and polite denial of systemic inequality, Kazemipur emphasizes that the Canadian *political system* is relatively constrained in its ability to act in an anti-Muslim fashion. In contrast, the Canadian *labour market* is largely unconstrained in its ability to act Islamophobically. Here Kazemipur points to significant disparities between Muslim and non-Muslim Canadians in the employment rate and average income, especially since 2011. Accordingly, he makes a case for stronger policy interventions around anti-Muslim bias in wage discrimination and hiring, in the process establishing a mandate for new audit studies and field experiments that can help specify how Islamophobia is operationalized in the labour market.

Notwithstanding Kazemipur's contribution, anti-Muslim behaviours in sites other than the labour market also require significant reform or even rebellion against the status quo. For example, it has now been established that CSIS and the RCMP have recently targeted Muslim Canadian university students—especially those in the elected leadership of campus student groups—for scrutiny, surveillance and intimidation (CBC News 2019a). This behaviour produces not only a chilling effect on the scholarship, advocacy and collective action that belongs at any healthy university but also heightens stress, harm and risk among community members. The important work that academic units like the University of Toronto's Institute for Islamic Studies are doing to offer pro-bono advice to affected students is exemplary, but warrantless surveillance and disregard for Muslims' rights go beyond a single campus. Evidence indicates that CSIS and the RCMP are systematically targeting Muslim university students across Canada (Global News 2018). Canadian faculty, especially tenure-track and tenured colleagues with significant employment protection, must speak out against the encroachment of state surveillance in all university classrooms and campuses. Moreover, those invested in building coalitions and strategies to counter anti-Muslim dehumanization must demand that the money and energy that has been expended on Muslim Canadian deradicalization should at least be matched by efforts to destabilize and deradicalize so-called "populist" groups. We must hold lawmakers accountable to holding industry partners in the tech sector accountable for the misinformation that circulates through their products. The same ingenuity and labour power that has designed technology to eavesdrop on private conversations and track people to determine which advertisements to place on their phone screens can surely be used to create tools that filter and purge racist, Islamophobic and antisemitic bots.

Akwasi Owusu-Bempah and Carl James' paper focuses on Black Canadians' negative perceptions of, and brutalizing treatment by, the state and its agents. The authors present evidence of anti-Black racism across the justice system, from police stop-and-search practices to racial disparities in pre-trial decision-making to widespread disrespect and undignified treatment of Black people as incarcerated subjects. Owusu-Bempah and James explain how in prisons, those who experience the most dehumanization integrate their observations of what happens to them into wide-ranging distrust and cynicism, which then reverberates into a pervasive and diffuse experience of dehumanization among Black Canadians in general.

Owusu-Bempah and James show how Black Canadians integrate their experience of dehumanization in the justice system into parallel dehumanization they have experienced in Canadian neighbourhoods, schools and other institutions marked by Black political disenfranchisement, social and economic disinvestment and state surveillance. Owusu-Bempah and James' expert legal testimony on anti-Black racism in cases involving systemic and social circumstances (R. v. Morris, 2018) and Owusu-Bempah's research advocacy around the expungement of convictions for cannabis-related crimes and his recommendation for reinvestment of tax revenues from legal sales of cannabis into communities harmed by over-policing are concrete examples of fighting anti-Black racism with evidence-based research.

Expanding on Owusu-Bempah and James' analysis, concerned citizens must better understand the experience of Black Canadians in all institutions where they experience racism and reform policy accordingly. Following the lead of generations of Black Canadian organizers, historians and scholars requires recognition that a full commitment to fighting anti-Black racism is intertwined with developing alternatives to prison. Incarceration should not be the go-to tool for building societal trust in social institutions and justice.

Restorative justice is one such alternative. It seeks to repair relationships and the harm caused by crime by bringing victims and offenders together. It gives victims a chance to describe the harm they suffered and offenders the opportunity to recognize the harm they have caused, apologize for it and provide restitution. Recent assessments show that restorative justice programs yield higher victim satisfaction, higher restitution compliance and lower recidivism than participating in a nonrestorative justice program does (Evans, McDonald and Gill 2018). As a society, we should commit to adapting such alternatives to prison for widest use, especially in communities that have been most harmed by over-policing and over-incarceration.

Owusu-Bempah and James' analysis also connects to research on the intersection of anti-Black racism, technology, and policing, where algorithms and innovations that are supposed to rid citizen-police encounters of their prejudice in fact bake anti-Black racism even deeper into systems of surveillance and punishment. For example, Amazon has aggressively marketed its Rekognition facial recognition tool to law enforcement at low cost, and it is now used by police departments in the United States and other countries. Yet independent tests of Amazon's tool show that the facial images it captures regularly produce false matches with mug shot databases and that a disproportionate number of these false matches involve faces with darker skin tones (ACLU 2018). For more than a year, Toronto Police were using similar facial recognition tools in a 2018 pilot project that was only recently disclosed to the public (CBC News 2019b). The Calgary police force uses the technology, while the Halifax and Montreal police forces refuse to say whether they are using it (Stop Facial Recognition in Canada 2020). Across Canada, we do not yet have laws that mediate or ban the use of facial recognition technologies. Concerned citizens must organize to stop their use—whether by law enforcement or for unsolicited commercial purposes—and put pressure on lawmakers to reform out-of-date federal privacy regulations.

Finally, Morton Weinfeld asks: Is antisemitism a permanent, cyclical fixture of Canadian society? How is Jewish-Canadian well-being targeted and undermined, and by whom? The United Nations' special rapporteur on religious beliefs recently delivered a searing interim report on the growth of antisemitism around the globe (UN General Assembly 2019). In 2018, the deadliest attack on Jews in the history of the United States occurred: the mass shooting at Pittsburgh's Tree of Life synagogue by a white supremacist with anti-immigration views. Weinfeld rightly laments the "new Canadian normal," where sites of worship are now securitized with armed guards and concrete slabs, and where vigilance reigns. The new Canadian normal also joins an invigorated transnational anti-Jewish discourse that has revived barely coded language like "globalism" and "cosmopolitanism" into a call for violent antisemitism. Across Canada we have witnessed an annual increase in antisemitic acts, especially harassment, but also involving the desecration of gravestones and the scrawling of anti-Jewish graffiti at synagogues, temples and schools.

Weinfeld ends his paper with several promising ideas for what can be done to curtail antisemitism today. His suggestion for continued collaboration between Jewish Canadians, other religious minorities and concerned members of dominant Christian or secular groups is especially compelling. Such collaboration could take the shape of locally meaningful and inclusive political action led by Jewish and Muslim partner organizations, such as advocacy and demonstration against laws that infringe on people's civil and religious liberties, like Quebec's Bill 21. It could also involve encouraging more interfaith prayer events and educational activities that facilitate what the European Jewish Congress calls "shared emotional experiences" that are "best suited to overcome religious hatred or immunize against it" (Lange et al. 2018: 39).

In a pluralistic society, preserving and sharing culturally specific stories and histories is an important mechanism for intergroup understanding and intragroup attachment. The contributions and stories of Jewish Canadians deserve further circulation in the arts, in our schools and across media channels. When thinking about the status of Jewish people in Canada today, we should recall that state-sanctioned bias against Jews was curtailed only in the second half of the twentieth century (Broadbent Institute 2017). Without romanticizing or flattening the complexity of this history, it could be useful to continue preserving and sharing the lessons of Jewish labour activists in the Canadian left, a major force in effecting this important social reform (Iacovetta, Draper and Ventresca 1998). As social and political actors, they successfully merged an "all boats will rise" ethos, which intentionally linked the fight against antisemitism with the fight against xenophobia, racism and class oppression, to their own discrete, meaningful and specifically Jewish cultural stories, scripts and registers. Based on how thoroughly this activism improved the material status of Jewish Canadians, including the eradication of quotas and barriers to Jewish inclusion in a variety of political, educational and industrial sectors, their stories and lesson might offer an important record for all Canadians who care about equality to revisit in the present political climate.

Religion, identity and group belonging can motivate exclusionary nationalist politics. However, spirituality, cultural specificity and affective communities can also be sites for transformational social justice. In the case of Jewish Canadians, this means we must continue to measure, study and mobilize the full diversity of bonds, feelings and commitments to politics that exist within and across the community. We must continue to demand that public and private educational institutions and memorials represent the fullest history of Jewish Canadian life. This includes an emphasis on and investment in curriculum that empowers learners to grapple with ethical and moral Jewish thought. We should encourage Jewish Canadians, who represent an incredibly diverse range of cultures, backgrounds and ethnicities, to narrate and lead such an effort.

The trajectories of Islamophobia, anti-Black racism and antisemitism in Canada are not linear or unidirectional. However, all three phenomena thrive on isolation, fear and fragmentation. By exercising empathy and redistributing or relinquishing resources and power to those who have been most harmed by present systems of oppression, we might be able to imagine and build a different future that fulfills the responsibility we owe this land and its inhabitants.

References

American Civil Liberties Union. 2018. Amazon's Face Recognition Falsely Matched 28 Members of Congress With Mugshots. July 26. https://www.aclu.org/blog/privacy-technology/surveillance-technologies/amazons-face-recognition-falsely-matched-28.

Anderson, B. 1991 [1983]. *Imagined Communities*. London: Verso.

Broadbent Institute. 2017. A legacy worth fighting for: the Left and the Jewish Community. 12 September. https://www.broadbentinstitute.ca/373252/a_legacy_worth_fighting_for_the_left_and_the_jewish_community.

CBC News. 2019a. When CSIS comes knocking: amid reports of Muslim students contacted by spy agency, hotline aims to help. 7 August. https://www.cbc.ca/news/canada/toronto/csis-students-university-muslim-campus-1.5229670.

_____. 2019b. Privacy advocates sound warning on Toronto police use of facial recognition technology. 30 May. https://www.cbc.ca/news/canada/toronto/privacy-civil-rights-concern-about-toronto-police-use-of-facial-recognition-1.5156581.

Clark, S.D. 1948. *Church and Sect in Canada*. Toronto: University of Toronto Press.

Evans, J., McDonald, S. and Gill, R. 2018. Restorative Justice: The Experiences of Victims and Survivors. *Victims of Crime Research Digest Number 11*. https://www.justice.gc.ca/eng/rp-pr/cj-jp/victim/rd11-rr11/p5.html.

Global News. 2018. Muslim students in Saskatchewan receiving calls from CSIS, say university Students. 20 November. https://globalnews.ca/news/4683333/muslim-students-saskatchewan-calls-csis/.

Iacovetta, F., Draper, P. and Ventresca, R. 1998. *A Nation of Immigrants: Women, Workers, and Communities in Canadian History, 1840s-1960s*. Toronto: University of Toronto Press.

Lange, A., Muzicant, A., Porat, D., Schiffman, L.H. and Weitzman, M. 2018. An End to Antisemitism! A Catalogue of Policies to Combat Antisemitism. *European Jewish Conference*. 13 December. https://eurojewcong.org/resources/catalogue-of-policies-for-combatting-antisemitism/.

Mills, C. 1997. *The Racial Contract*. Ithaca NY: Cornell University Press.

Stop Facial Recognition in Canada. 2020. https://act.openmedia.org/StopFacialRecognition .

United Nations General Assembly. 2019. Elimination of all forms of religious intolerance. Document A/74/358, 30 September. https://undocs.org/A/74/358.

Wimmer, A. and Glick-Schiller, N. 2003. Methodological Nationalism, the Social Sciences, and the Study of Migration: An Essay in Historical Epistemology. *International Migration Review* 37(3): 576–610.

Contributors

Robert Brym is S.D. Clark Professor of Sociology at the University of Toronto and a Fellow of the Royal Society of Canada. He has won numerous awards for his research and teaching, including the *British Journal of Sociology* Prize, the Northrop Frye Prize and the Outstanding Contribution Award of the Canadian Sociology and Anthropology Association. He has published widely on politics and ethnic relations in Russia, the Middle East and Canada. For details and downloadable publications, visit https://utoronto.academia. edu/.

Carl E. James is Jean Augustine Chair in Education, Community and Diaspora at York University, Founding Director of the York Centre for Education and Community and a Fellow of the Royal Society of Canada. He is widely recognized for his work in ethnically and racially diverse communities and for his role, nationally and internationally, in research on equity and identity as they relate to race, class, gender, racialization, immigration and citizenship. He has won numerous awards for his work, including the William P. Hubbard Award for Race Relations, the African Canadian Achievement Award and the Harry Jerome Award. His most recent book is *Life at the Intersection: Community, Class and Schooling* (Fernwood, 2012), a study of the Jane and Finch neighbourhood in Toronto's north end.

Abdie Kazemipur is Professor of Sociology, Chair of Ethnic Studies and Academic Director of the Prairie Regional Research Data Centre at the University of Calgary. His research is on the socio-economic experience of immigrants in Canada and socio-cultural developments in the Middle East. He is the recipient of the 2015 John Porter Award of the Canadian Sociological Association for *The Muslim Question in Canada* (UBC Press, 2014) and the 2018 National Metropolis Researcher Award for his contributions to immigration research in Canada. His most recent book, on religious developments in Iran, is currently under review. For more information, visit www. abdiekazemipur.com.

Neda Maghbouleh is Assistant Professor of Sociology and Canada Research Chair in Migration, Race and Identity at the University of Toronto Mississauga. Her scholarship brings together the study of international migration and race/ethnicity to learn how refugees and immigrants from the Middle East navigate new worlds in North America. A recent recipient of the Province of Ontario's Early Researcher Award, she is author of the award-winning *The Limits of Whiteness: Iranian Americans and the Everyday Politics of Race* (Stanford University Press, 2017). Her publications are available at www.nedamaghbouleh.com.

Akwasi Owusu-Bempah is an Assistant Professor in the Department of Sociology at the University of Toronto and a Senior Fellow at Massey College. Trained as a criminologist, he conducts research on the intersection of race, crime and criminal justice, with a particular interest in policing. His current projects include a study of Black males' perceptions of and experiences with the police in the Greater Toronto Area and an examination of representations of Blackness in Canadian print media. He is also studying various aspects of cannabis legalization in Canada. His research has recently been published in *Policing and Society*, *Crime and Justice*, and *Theoretical Criminology*. He has also provided a range of consultative services to various levels of government.

Morton Weinfeld is Professor of Sociology at McGill University, where he holds the Chair in Canadian Ethnic Studies. He has published widely on the sociology of Canadian Jewry and more generally on Canadian diversity, immigration, inequality and multiculturalism. The first edition of his *Like Everyone Else, but Different: The Paradoxical Success of Canadian Jews* (McClelland & Stewart, 2002) won the J.I. Segal Award, the Canadian Jewish Book Award and the Lockshin-Frances and Samuel Stein Memorial Prize for Scholarship on a Canadian Jewish Theme, and was nominated for a Quebec Writer's Federation Award. (A second edition, with R.F. Schnoor and M. Shames, was published by McGill-Queen's University Press in 2018.) See www.mcgill.ca/sociology/faculty/weinfeld for a list of publications.

Index

Proceedings of the S.D. Clark Symposium on the Future of Canadian Society

of residential segregation. The first S.D. Clark Symposium picked up where Clark left off by focusing on income inequality and its implications. Contributors include Robert Andersen, Lars Osberg, Ito Peng, Gordon Cleveland, John Myles, and Emily Laxer, with Robert Brym's introduction providing an overview of the subject.